The Upward

A Reader For Colored Children

Mary White Ovington, Myron T. Pritchard

Alpha Editions

This edition published in 2024

ISBN : 9789362090478

Design and Setting By
Alpha Editions
www.alphaedis.com
Email - info@alphaedis.com

Contents

FOREWORD

To the present time, there has been no collection of stories and poems by Negro writers, which colored children could read with interest and pleasure and in which they could find a mirror of the traditions and aspirations of their race. Realizing this lack, Myron T. Pritchard, Principal of the Everett School, Boston, and Mary White Ovington, Chairman of the Board of the National Association for the Advancement of Colored People, have brought together poems, stories, sketches and addresses which bear eloquent testimony to the richness of the literary product of our Negro writers. It is the hope that this little book will find a large welcome in all sections of the country and will bring good cheer and encouragement to the young readers who have so largely the fortunes of their race in their own hands.

The editors desire to express thanks to the authors who have generously granted the use of their work. Especial acknowledgement is due to Mrs. Booker T. Washington for the selection from *Up from Slavery*; to *The Crisis* for "The Rondeau," by Jessie Fauset, "The Brave Son," by Alston W. Burleigh, "The Black Fairy," by Fenton Johnson, "The Children at Easter," by C. Emily Frazier, "His Motto," by Lottie B. Dixon, "Negro Soldiers," by Roscoe C. Jamison, "A Legend of the Blue Jay," by Ruth Anna Fisher; to the American Book Company for "The Dog and the Clever Rabbit," from *Animal Tales*, by A. O. Stafford; to Frederick A. Stokes and Company for "A Negro Explorer at the North Pole," by Matthew A. Henson; to A. C. McClurg and Company for the selection from *Souls of Black Folk*, by W. E. B. DuBois; to Henry Holt and Company for the selection from *The Negro*, by W. E. B. DuBois; to the Cornhill Company for the selections from The *Band of Gideon*, by Joseph F. Cotter, Jr., and *The Menace of the South*, by William J. Edwards; to Dodd, Mead and Company for "Ere Sleep Comes Down" and the "Boy and the Bayonet" (copyright 1907), by Paul Laurence Dunbar.

INTRODUCTION

The Negro has been in America just about three hundred years and in that time he has become intertwined in all the history of the nation. He has fought in her wars; he has endured hardships with her pioneers; he has toiled in her fields and factories; and the record of some of the nation's greatest heroes is in large part the story of their service and sacrifice for this people.

The Negro arrived in America as a slave in 1619, just one year before the Pilgrims arrived at Plymouth in search of freedom. Since then their lot has not always been a happy one, but nevertheless, in spite of difficulties and hardships, the race has learned many valuable lessons in its conflict with the American civilization. As a slave the lessons of labor, of constructive endeavor, of home-life and religion were learned, even if the opportunity was not always present to use these lessons to good advantage.

After slavery other lessons were learned in their order. Devoted self-sacrificing souls—soldiers of human brotherhood—took up the task in the schoolroom which their brothers began on the battlefield. Here it was that the Negro learned the history of America, of the deeds of her great men, the stirring events which marked her development, the ideals that made America great. And so well have they been learned, that to-day there are no more loyal Americans than the twelve million Negroes that make up so large a part of the nation.

But the race has other things yet to learn: The education of any race is incomplete unless the members of that race know the history and character of its own people as well as those of other peoples. The Negro has yet to learn of the part which his own race has played in making America great; has yet to learn of the noble and heroic souls among his own people, whose achievements are praiseworthy among any people. A number of books— poetry, history and fiction—have been written by Negro authors in which the life of their own people has been faithfully and attractively set forth; but until recently no effort has been made on a large scale to see that Negro boys and girls became acquainted with these books and the facts they contained concerning their people.

In this volume the publishers have brought together a number of selections from the best literary works of Negro authors, through which these young people may learn more of the character and accomplishments of the worthy members of their race. Such matter is both informing and inspiring, and no Negro boy or girl can read it without feeling a deeper pride in his own race. The selections are each calculated to teach a valuable lesson, and all make a direct appeal to the best impulses of the human heart.

For a number of years several educational institutions for Negro youths have conducted classes in Negro history with a similar object in view. The results of these classes have been most gratifying and the present volume is a commendable contribution to the literature of such a course.

ROBERT R. MOTON

TUSKEGEE INSTITUTE, ALA.,
June 30, 1920

To the man in the tower the world below him is likely to look very small. Men look like ants and all the bustle and stir of their hurrying lives seems pitifully confused and aimless. But the man in the street who is looking and striving upward is in a different situation. However poor his present plight, the thing he aims at and is striving toward stands out clear and distinct above him, inspiring him with hope and ambition in his struggle upward. For the man who is down there is always something to hope for, always something to be gained. The man who is down, looking up, may catch a glimpse now and then of heaven, but the man who is so situated that he can only look down is pretty likely to see another and quite different place.

BOOKER T. WASHINGTON

THE BOY AND THE BAYONET

PAUL LAURENCE DUNBAR

It was June, and nearing the closing time of school. The air was full of the sound of bustle and preparation for the final exercises, field day, and drills. Drills especially, for nothing so gladdens the heart of the Washington mother, be she black or white, as seeing her boy in the blue cadet's uniform, marching proudly to the huzzas of an admiring crowd. Then she forgets the many nights when he has come in tired out and dusty from his practice drill, and feels only the pride and elation of the result.

Although Tom did all he could outside of study hours, there were many days of hard work for Hannah Davis, when her son went into the High School. But she took it upon herself gladly, since it gave Bud the chance to learn, that she wanted him to have. When, however, he entered the Cadet Corps it seemed to her as if the first steps toward the fulfilment of all her hopes had been made. It was a hard pull to her, getting the uniform, but Bud himself helped manfully, and when his mother saw him rigged out in all his regimentals, she felt that she had not toiled in vain. And in fact it was worth all the trouble and expense just to see the joy and pride of "little sister," who adored Bud.

As the time for the competitive drill drew near there was an air of suppressed excitement about the little house on "D" Street, where the three lived. All day long "little sister," who was never very well and did not go to school, sat and looked out of the window on the uninteresting prospect of a dusty thoroughfare lined on either side with dull red brick houses, all of the same ugly pattern, interspersed with older, uglier, and viler frame shanties. In the evening Hannah hurried home to get supper against the time when Bud should return, hungry and tired from his drilling, and the chore work which followed hard upon its heels.

Things were all cheerful, however, for as they applied themselves to the supper, the boy, with glowing face, would tell just how his company "A" was getting on, and what they were going to do to companies "B" and "C." It was not boasting so much as the expression of a confidence, founded upon the hard work he was doing, and Hannah and the "little sister" shared that with him.

The child often, listening to her brother, would clap her hands or cry, "Oh, Bud, you're just splendid an' I know you'll beat 'em."

"If hard work'll beat 'em, we've got 'em beat," Bud would reply, and Hannah, to add an admonitory check to her own confidence, would break in with, "Now, don't you be too sho'; dey ain't been no man so good dat dey wasn't somebody bettah." But all the while her face and manner were disputing what her words expressed.

The great day came, and it was a wonderful crowd of people that packed the great baseball grounds to overflowing. It seemed that all of Washington's colored population was out, when there were really only about one-tenth of them there. It was an enthusiastic, banner-waving, shouting, hallooing crowd. Its component parts were strictly and frankly partisan, and so separated themselves into sections differentiated by the colors of the flags they carried and the ribbons they wore. Side yelled defiance at side, and party bantered party. Here the blue and white of company "A" flaunted audaciously on the breeze beside the very seats over which the crimson and gray of "B" were flying and they in their turn nodded defiance over the imaginary barrier between themselves and "C's" black and yellow.

The band was thundering out Sousa's "High School Cadet's March," the school officials, the judges, and reporters, and some with less purpose were bustling about discussing and conferring. Altogether doing nothing much with beautiful unanimity. All was noise, hurry, gaiety, and turbulence.

In the midst of it all, with blue and white rosettes pinned on their breasts, sat two spectators, tense and silent, while the breakers of movement and sound struck and broke around them. It seemed too much to Hannah and "little sister" for them to laugh and shout. Bud was with company "A," and so the whole program was more like a religious ceremonial to them. The blare of the brass to them might have been the trumpet call to battle in old Judea, and the far-thrown tones of the megaphone the voice of a prophet proclaiming from the hill-top.

Hannah's face glowed with expectation, and "little sister" sat very still and held her mother's hand save when amid a burst of cheers company "A" swept into the parade ground at a quick step, then she sprang up, crying shrilly, "There's Bud! there's Bud! I see him!" and then settled back into her seat overcome with embarrassment. The mother's eyes danced as soon as the sister's had singled out their dear one from the midst of the blue-coated boys, and it was an effort for her to keep from following her little daughter's example even to echoing her words.

Company "A" came swinging down the field toward the judges in a manner that called for more enthusiastic huzzas that carried even the Freshmen of other commands "off their feet." They were, indeed, a set of fine-looking young fellows, brisk, straight, and soldierly in bearing. Their captain was proud of them, and his very step showed it. He was like a skilled operator pressing the key of some great mechanism, and at his command they moved like clockwork. Seen from the side it was as if they were all bound together by inflexible iron bars, and as the end man moved all must move with him.

The crowd was full of exclamations of praise and admiration, but a tense quiet enveloped them as company "A" came from columns of four into line for volley firing. This was a real test; it meant not only grace and precision of movement, singleness of attention and steadiness, but quickness tempered by self-control. At the command the volley rang forth like a single shot. This was again the signal for wild cheering and the blue and white streamers kissed the sunlight with swift impulsive kisses. Hannah and "little sister" drew closer together and pressed hands.

The "A" adherents, however, were considerably cooled when the next volley came out, badly scattering, with one shot entirely apart and before the rest. Bud's mother did not entirely understand the sudden quieting of the adherents; they felt vaguely that all was not as it should be, and the chill of fear laid hold upon their hearts. What if Bud's company (it was always Bud's company to them), what if his company should lose. But, of course, that couldn't be. Bud himself had said that they would win. Suppose, though, they didn't; and with these thoughts they were miserable until the cheering again told them that the company had redeemed itself.

Someone behind Hannah said, "They are doing splendidly, they'll win, they'll win yet in spite of the second volley."

Company "A," in columns of four, had executed the right oblique in double time, and halted amid cheers; then formed left front into line without halting. The next movement was one looked forward to with much anxiety on account of its difficulty. The order was marching by fours to fix or unfix bayonets. They were going at a quick step, but the boys' hands were steady—hope was bright in their hearts. They were doing it rapidly and freely, when suddenly from the ranks there was the bright gleam of steel lower down than it should have been. A gasp broke from the breasts of company "A's" friends. The blue and white dropped disconsolately, while a few heartless ones who wore other colors attempted to hiss. Someone had dropped his bayonet. But with muscles unquivering, without a turned head, the company moved on as if nothing had happened, while one of the judges, an army officer, stepped into the wake of the boys and picked up the fallen steel.

No two eyes had seen half so quickly as Hannah and "little sister's" who the blunderer was. In the whole drill there had been but one figure for them, and that was Bud,—Bud, and it was he who had dropped his bayonet. Anxious, nervous with the desire to please them, perhaps with a shade too much of thought of them looking on with their hearts in their eyes, he had fumbled, and lost all he was striving for. His head went round and round and all seemed black before him.

He executed the movements in a dazed way. The applause, generous and sympathetic, as his company left the parade ground, came to him from afar off, and like a wounded animal he crept away from his comrades, not because their reproaches stung him, for he did not hear them, but because he wanted to think what his mother and "little sister" would say, but his misery was as nothing to that of the two who sat up there amid the ranks of the blue and white, holding each other's hands with a despairing grip. To Bud all of the rest of the contest was a horrid nightmare; he hardly knew when the three companies were marched back to receive the judges' decision. The applause that greeted company "B" when the blue ribbons were pinned on the members' coats meant nothing to his ears. He had disgraced himself and his company. What would his mother and his "little sister" say?

To Hannah and "little sister," as to Bud, all of the remainder of the drill was a misery. The one interest they had had in it failed, and not even the dropping of his gun by one of company "E" when on the march, halting in line, could raise their spirits. The little girl tried to be brave, but when it was all over she was glad to hurry out before the crowd got started and to hasten away home. Once there and her tears flowed freely; she hid her face in her mother's dress, and sobbed as if her heart would break.

"Don't cry, Baby! don't cry, Lammie, dis ain't da las' time da wah goin' to be a drill. Bud'll have a chance anotha time and den he'll show 'em somethin'; bless you, I spec' he'll be a captain." But this consolation of philosophy was nothing to "little sister." It was so terrible to her, this failure of Bud's. She couldn't blame him, she couldn't blame anyone else, and she had not yet learned to lay all such unfathomed catastrophes at the door of fate. What to her was the thought of another day; what did it matter to her whether he was a captain or a private? She didn't even know the meaning of the words, but "little sister," from the time she knew Bud was a private, thought that was much better than being a captain or any other of those things with a long name, so that settled it.

Her mother finally set about getting the supper, while "little sister" drooped disconsolately in her own little splint-bottomed chair. She sat there weeping silently until she heard the sound of Bud's step, then sprang up and ran away to hide. She didn't dare to face him with tears in her eyes. Bud came in without a word and sat down in the dark front room.

"Dat you, Bud?" asked his mother.

"Yassum."

"Bettah come now, supper's puty 'nigh ready."

"I don't want no supper."

"You bettah come on, Bud, I reckon you's mighty tired."

He did not reply, but just then a pair of thin arms were put around his neck and a soft cheek was placed close to his own.

"Come on, Buddie," whispered "little sister," "Mammy an' me know you didn't mean to do it, an' we don't keer."

Bud threw his arms around his little sister and held her tightly.

"It's only you an' ma I care about," he said, "though I am sorry I spoiled the company's drill; they say "B" would have won anyway on account of our bad firing, but I did want you and ma to be proud."

"We is proud," she whispered, "we's mos' prouder dan if you'd won," and pretty soon she led him by the hand to supper.

Hannah did all she could to cheer the boy and to encourage him to hope for next year, but he had little to say in reply, and went to bed early.

In the morning, though it neared school time, Bud lingered around and seemed in no disposition to get ready to go.

"Bettah git ready fer school," said Hannah cheerily.

"I don't believe I want to go any more," Bud replied.

"Not go any more? Why, ain't you 'shamed to talk that way! O' cose you goin' to school."

"I'm ashamed to show my face to the boys."

"What you say about de boys? De boys ain't a-goin' to give you an edgication when you need it."

"Oh, I don't want to go, ma; you don't know how I feel."

"I'm kinder sorry I let you go into dat company," said Hannah musingly, "'cause it was de teachin' I wanted you to git, not the prancin' and steppin'; but I did t'ink it would make mo' of a man of you, an' it ain't. Yo' pappy was a po' man, ha'd wo'kin', an' he wasn't high-toned neither, but from the time I first see him to the day of his death, I nevah seen him back down because he was afeared of anything," and Hannah turned to her work.

"Little sister" went up and slipped her hand in his. "You ain't a-goin to back down, is you, Buddie?" she said.

"No," said Bud stoutly, as he braced his shoulders, "I'm a-goin'."

But no persuasion could make him wear his uniform.

The boys were a little cold to him, and some were brutal. But most of them recognized the fact that what had happened to Tom Harris might have happened to any one of them. Besides, since the percentage had been shown, it was found that "B" had outpointed them in many ways, and so their loss was not due to the one grave error.

Bud's heart sank when he dropped into his seat in the Assembly Hall to find seated on the platform one of the blue-coated officers who had acted as judge the day before. After the opening exercises were over he was called upon to address the school. He spoke readily and pleasantly, laying especial stress upon the value of discipline; toward the end of his address he said "I suppose company 'A' is heaping accusations upon the head of the young man who dropped his bayonet yesterday." Tom could have died. "It was most regrettable," the officer continued, "but to me the most significant thing at the drill was the conduct of that cadet afterward. I saw the whole proceeding; I saw that he did not pause for an instant, that he did not even turn his head, and it appeared to me as one of the finest bits of self-control I had ever seen in any youth; had he forgotten himself for a moment and stopped, however quickly, to secure the weapon, the next line would have been interfered with and your whole movement thrown into confusion." There were a half hundred eyes glancing furtively at Bud, and the light began to dawn in his face. "This boy has shown what discipline means, and I for one want to shake hands with him, if he is here."

When he had concluded the Principal called Bud forward, and the boys, even his detractors, cheered as the officer took his hand.

"Why are you not in uniform, sir?" he asked.

"I was ashamed to wear it after yesterday," was the reply.

"Don't be ashamed to wear your uniform," the officer said to him, and Bud could have fallen on his knees and thanked him.

There were no more jeers from his comrades, and when he related it all at home that evening there were two more happy hearts in that South Washington cottage.

"I told you we was more prouder dan if you'd won," said "little sister."

"An' what did I tell you 'bout backin' out?" asked his mother.

Bud was too happy and too busy to answer; he was brushing his uniform.

THE BEGINNINGS OF A MISSISSIPPI SCHOOL

WILLIAM H. HOLTZCLAW

I had been unable to get permission to teach in the little church, so I started my school in the open air. We were out under the big trees amidst the shrubbery. This would have made a very good schoolhouse but for its size. In such a schoolhouse one could get along very well, if he could keep his pupils close enough to him, but the chances are, as I have found, that they will put bugs down one another's collars, and while you are hearing one class the other children will chase one another about. Their buoyant spirits will not permit them to keep quiet while they are in the open. It is pretty hard to hear a class reciting and at the same time to witness a boxing-match, but those who teach in the open air must be prepared for such performances. These annoyances were accentuated by the fact that some of my pupils were forty years old while others were six.

After a while we moved into an abandoned house, which we used for a schoolhouse, but it was little better than teaching out of doors. When it rained the water not only came through the roof, but through the sides as well. During cold winter rains I had to teach while standing with my overcoat on and with arctic rubbers to protect myself against pneumonia. During those rainy days Miss Lee, my assistant, would get up on a bench and stand there all day to keep her feet out of the water and would have an umbrella stretched over her to keep from getting wet from above. The little fellows would be standing in the water below like little ducks. They stood these conditions exceedingly well. Many of them were not protected with overshoes or any shoes, but they came to school each day just as if they had been properly clad.

It is impossible to describe the hardships that we suffered during that winter, which was severe for the South. As the winter came on and grew more and more severe a great many of the children were taken with pneumonia, la grippe, and similar ailments. I wished, in the interest of health, to abandon the school for a few weeks until better weather; but neither pupils, nor teachers, nor parents would listen to this, and so the school continued under these circumstances until the new schoolhouse was ready for use. It is needless to say that some of the pupils never survived those conditions; in fact, the strange thing is that any of us did.

UP FROM SLAVERY

THE STRUGGLE FOR AN EDUCATION

BOOKER T. WASHINGTON

One day, while at work in the coal-mine, I happened to overhear two miners talking about a great school for colored people somewhere in Virginia. This was the first time that I had ever heard anything about any kind of school or college that was more pretentious than the little colored school in our town.

In the darkness of the mine I noiselessly crept as close as I could to the two men who were talking. I heard one tell the other that not only was the school established for the members of my race, but that opportunities were provided by which poor but worthy students could work out all or a part of the cost of board, and at the same time be taught some trade or industry.

As they went on describing the school, it seemed to me that it must be the greatest place on earth, and not even Heaven presented more attractions for me at that time than did the Hampton Normal and Agricultural Institute in Virginia, about which these men were talking. I resolved at once to go to that school, although I had no idea where it was, or how many miles away, or how I was going to reach it; I remembered only that I was on fire constantly with one ambition, and that was to go to Hampton. This thought was with me day and night.

After hearing of the Hampton Institute, I continued to work for a few months longer in the coal-mine. While at work there, I heard of a vacant position in the household of General Lewis Ruffner, the owner of the salt-furnace and coal-mine. Mrs. Viola Ruffner, the wife of General Ruffner, was a "Yankee" woman from Vermont. Mrs. Ruffner had a reputation all through the vicinity for being very strict with her servants, and especially with the boys who tried to serve her. Few of them had remained with her more than two or three weeks. They all left with the same excuse: she was too strict. I decided, however, that I would rather try Mrs. Ruffner's house than remain in the coal-mine, and so my mother applied to her for the vacant position. I was hired at a salary of $5 per month.

I had heard so much about Mrs. Ruffner's severity that I was almost afraid to see her, and trembled when I went into her presence. I had not lived with her many weeks, however, before I began to understand her. I soon began to learn that, first of all, she wanted everything kept clean about her, that she wanted things done promptly and systematically, and that at the bottom of everything she wanted absolute honesty and frankness. Nothing must be sloven or slipshod; every door, every fence, must be kept in repair.

I cannot now recall how long I lived with Mrs. Ruffner before going to Hampton, but I think it must have been a year and a half. At any rate, I here repeat what I have said more than once before, that the lessons that I learned in the home of Mrs. Ruffner were as valuable to me as any education I have ever gotten anywhere since. Even to this day I never see bits of paper scattered around a house or in the street that I do not want to pick them up at once. I never see a filthy yard that I do not want to clean it, a paling off of a fence that I do not want to put it on, an unpainted or unwhitewashed house that I do not want to paint or whitewash it, or a button off one's clothes, or a grease-spot on them or on a floor, that I do not want to call attention to it.

From fearing Mrs. Ruffner I soon learned to look upon her as one of my best friends. When she found that she could trust me she did so implicitly. During the one or two winters that I was with her she gave me an opportunity to go to school for an hour in the day during a portion of the winter months, but most of my studying was done at night, sometimes alone, sometimes under some one whom I could hire to teach me. Mrs. Ruffner always encouraged and sympathized with me in all my efforts to get an education. It was while living with her that I began to get together my first library. I secured a dry-goods box, knocked out one side of it, put some shelves in it, and began putting into it every kind of book that I could get my hands upon, and called it "my library."

Without any unusual occurrence I reached Hampton, with a surplus of exactly fifty cents with which to begin my education. To me it had been a long, eventful journey; but the first sight of the large, three-story, brick school building seemed to have rewarded me for all that I had undergone in order to reach the place. If the people who gave the money to provide that building could appreciate the influence the sight of it had upon me, as well as upon thousands of other youths, they would feel all the more encouraged to make such gifts. It seemed to me to be the largest and most beautiful building I had ever seen. The sight of it seemed to give me new life. I felt that a new kind of existence had now begun—that life would now have a new meaning. I felt that I had reached the promised land, and I resolved to let no obstacle prevent me from putting forth the highest effort to fit myself to accomplish the most good in the world.

As soon as possible after reaching the grounds of the Hampton Institute, I presented myself before the head teacher for assignment to a class. Having been so long without proper food, a bath, and change of clothing, I did not, of course, make a very favorable impression upon her, and I could see at once that there were doubts in her mind about the wisdom of admitting me as a student. I felt that I could hardly blame her if she got the idea that I was a worthless loafer or tramp. For some time she did not refuse to admit me, neither did she decide in my favor, and I continued to linger about her, and to impress her in all the ways I could with my worthiness. In the meantime I saw her admitting other students, and that added greatly to my discomfort, for I felt, deep down in my heart, that I could do as well as they, if I could only get a chance to show what was in me.

After some hours had passed, the head teacher said to me, "The adjoining recitation room needs sweeping. Take the broom and sweep it."

It occurred to me at once that here was my chance. Never did I receive an order with more delight. I knew that I could sweep, for Mrs. Ruffner had thoroughly taught me how to do that when I lived with her.

I swept the recitation-room three times. Then I got a dusting-cloth and I dusted it four times. All the woodwork around the walls, every bench, table, and desk, I went over four times with my dusting-cloth. Besides, every piece of furniture had been moved and every closet and corner in the room had been thoroughly cleaned. I had the feeling that in a large measure my future depended upon the impression I made upon the teacher in the cleaning of that room. When I was through, I reported to the head teacher. She was a "Yankee" woman who knew just where to look for dirt. She went into the room and inspected the floor and closets; then she took her handkerchief and rubbed it on the wood-work about the walls, and over the table and benches. When she was unable to find one bit of dirt on the floor, or a particle of dust on any of the furniture, she remarked quietly, "I guess you will do to enter this institution."

BOOKER T. WASHINGTON

A STUDENT'S MEMORY OF HIM

WILLIAM H. HOLTZCLAW

One thing about Mr. Washington that impressed me was his regularity. He was as regular as the clock. He appeared at his office in the morning exactly at eight o'clock, remained until twelve, very often took part in an Executive Council meeting until one, and then went to lunch. At two o'clock he would again be in his office and would invariably remain there until half-past four, when he would leave and tramp across the plantation; sometimes he would run for a mile or two, as fast as he could go, for exercise. When he returned he would go to his library and there would pass the time until six, when he would go to dinner. After dinner he played with the children for a while and then returned to his library until 8.40. He would then go to Chapel for evening prayers with the whole student body. This prayer service was one that Mr. Washington seldom ever missed and he always appeared on the rostrum exactly on the minute.

Mr. Washington had a grasp of the details of the work of Tuskegee that seemed almost incredible. I remember one evening that I was startled to hear my name, together with that of one of my friends, called out by Mr. Washington from the chapel platform. He simply said, "William Holtzclaw and Charles Washington may rise." I was so weak in my knees that I could scarcely stand, but I knew nothing else to do but to rise at the command of that voice. After we stood up and the whole school was looking at us, Mr. Washington said: "These young men may pass out of the Chapel and go and pick up the tools they worked with to-day." We had been ditching and when the work-bell rang had left our tools where we were working, when they should have been carried to the toolhouse.

If the water main, or water pipe, had a defect in it so that it was leaking anywhere on the grounds, Mr. Washington was almost sure to see that something was wrong and to call the matter to the attention of the Superintendent of Industries.

If he came into the dining-room while the students were eating their meals, he would notice such small details as a student's pouring out more molasses on his plate than he could eat and would stop in the dining-room, send for the matron, have some bread brought to the student, and wait until that student had eaten all the molasses he had poured on his plate.

If one walked about the campus at night, he would be sure to meet Mr. Washington almost anywhere on the grounds. For instance, he might be found in the kitchen at two o'clock in the morning examining the method of preparing the students' breakfast. He seldom seemed to me to take sufficient rest for an average man.

ANNA-MARGARET

AUGUSTA BIRD

To Anna-Margaret's mind, being the baby of the family was simply awful. This fact seemed to grow with it each day. It began in the morning when she watched her sisters as they laughed and rollicked through their dressing.

"Bet I'll beat, and you got on your stockings already," challenged Edith.

"I'll bet you won't,—bet I'll be out to the pump, my face washed, and be at the breakfast table and you won't have your shoes laced up," boasted Ruth, the older of the two.

"We'll see, we'll see," giggled Edith.

"Oho, I guess you will. Mother gave you new shoe strings," said Ruth somewhat crestfallen.

"I told you so, I told you so," and Edith bounded out of the door, closely pursued by Ruth who cried: "You didn't beat me but 'bout an inch."

Anna-Margaret was left alone to sit and think for all the next hour how perfectly awful it was to be the baby, until Mother Dear was able to come and dress her.

The next morning it was the same torture all over again. It seemed to Anna-Margaret that people never stopped to think or know what a baby was forced to go through. There were Edith and Ruth racing again. Anna-Margaret spied her shoes and stockings on a chair. Out of the side of her crib she climbed.

"Look at Anna-Margaret!" screamed Edith.

"You, Anna-Margaret, get right back in that crib!" commanded Ruth assuming her mother's tone.

"I won't!" And right over to the chair where her shoes and stockings were, walked the baby. She seated herself on the floor and drew on her stocking as if she had been in the habit of doing it on preceding mornings. It was surprising to Anna-Margaret, herself, the ease with which it went on.

"Look at that child," gasped Ruth.

Edith looked and said a little grudgingly, "I'll bet she can't put on her shoes though." Edith remembered how long it was before she was able to put on her shoes, and this accomplishment, in her mind, seemed to give her a great superiority over her baby sister.

"Come on, Edith," called Ruth, "I'll beat you down to the pump and I'll give you to the rose bush, too."

Struggling, pulling and twisting sat Anna-Margaret all alone, but the shoe would not go on. She was just about to give up in utter despair and burst into tears when Mother Dear appeared in the doorway.

"What is mother's angel doing? Well, well, look at Mother's smart child, she has got on her stocking already,—here, let mother help her."

It was awful to think you were still such a baby that you couldn't do anything yourself, but it was very nice, so Anna-Margaret thought, to have such an adorable mother to come to your rescue.

"There now, run out and tell Ruth to wash your face and then mother will give you your breakfast."

"Wash my face, Ruth," requested Anna-Margaret at the pump.

"Who laced up your shoes?" asked Edith suspiciously.

"I did." Anna-Margaret said it so easily that it startled herself.

"I don't believe it, I don't believe it. I am going to ask Mother."

"Hold still, will you, and let me wash your face," commanded Ruth.

As soon as she was free, away went Anna-Margaret back to the house.

"Muvver, Muvver," cried Anna-Margaret almost breathless as she entered the big kitchen, "tell Edith I laced up my shoes, tell 'er, Muvver, will yo', Muvver?"

Mother stopped her work at the breakfast table. "Anna-Margaret, I could not do that because you didn't."

"But tell 'er I did, won't you, Muvver," she pleaded.

"Anna-Margaret, I can't do that because I would be telling a lie. Don't I whip Ruth and Edith for telling lies?"

"Tell a lie, Muvver, tell a lie, *I won't whip you.*"

Mother Dear was forced to smile. "Here, eat your breakfast, I can't promise my baby I will tell a lie, even if she won't whip me."

Fortunately no one questioned Mother Dear and Anna-Margaret ate her breakfast in silence. Then kissing her mother in a matter of fact way, she went out to play with her sisters.

"Ah, here comes Anna-Margaret to knock down our things," moaned Edith.

"Let her come on," cried Ruth, "and we'll go down in the bottom and build sand forts; it rained yesterday and the sand is nice and damp."

"Oh-oo, let's," echoed Edith, and off they scampered. Anna-Margaret saw them and started after them as fast as her little chubby brown legs could carry her, which wasn't very fast. The other children were far in front of her. Anna-Margaret stopped suddenly,—she heard a little biddie in distress. There was a mother hen darting through the grass after a fleeing grasshopper, and close behind her was the whole flock save one. Anna-Margaret watched them as the young chickens spread open their wings and hurried in pursuit of their mother. Far behind one little black, fuzzy biddie struggled and tripped over the tall grass stems. The baby looked at the little chick and then at the other ones and saw that they were different. She didn't know what the difference was. She could not understand that the other chickens were several days older and that this one had only been taken away from its own mother hen that morning in order that she would remain on her nest until all her chicks were hatched. All Anna-Margaret knew was that they were different.

"Poor l'll biddie, dey don't want you to play wif them," she sympathized, "come, come to Anna-Margaret."

With little difficulty she captured the young chick and started back to the house.

"Dat's all 'ight, I know what I'm gonna do," she decided, "I'm gonna play Dod. Poor l'll biddie, just wait, Anna-Margaret'll fix yo', so you can run and fly and keep up with the biddies. Won't dat be nice, uh?" And she put her curly head down close to the little chick as if to catch its answer.

Anna-Margaret went straight to the big sewing-basket and placing the biddie on the machine extracted a threaded needle. Cutting two small pieces of black cloth for wings, she took the chick and seated herself on the drop-step between the sewing-room and dining-room. She then attempted to sew one of the little black pieces of cloth to one of the tiny wings of the young chick.

"There, there, yo'll be all 'ight in dest a minute," she said amid the distressful chirping of the chick. The biddie's cries brought Mother Dear to the scene.

"Anna-Margaret, what on earth are you doing to the little chicken?"

Anna-Margaret turned her big brown eyes upon her mother. "I'm playin' Dod and I'm puttin' some wings on des l'll biddie so it can run and fly like the oo-ver ones, and so they won't run off all the time and leave it."

"But Anna-Margaret, don't you know you are hurting the little biddie?"

"No-o, Muvver," she said slowly, "but I know what it is to be always runned off and lef'."

Mother Dear understood what was in her baby's mind as she gathered her up in her arms. Anna-Margaret dropped the sewing, cuddled the little biddie close in one arm and clasped her mother's neck with the other. Mother Dear held her closely.

"I love yo', Muvver Dear," whispered Anna-Margaret.

"I love you, baby dear," was the whispered answer.

Being the baby of the family to Anna-Margaret's mind, just now, was awfully nice.

CHARITY

H. CORDELIA RAY

I saw a maiden, fairest of the fair,
With every grace bedight beyond compare.
Said I, "What doest thou, pray, tell to me!"
"I see the good in others," answered she.

MY FIRST SCHOOL

W. E. B. DUBOIS

Once upon a time I taught school in the hills of Tennessee, where the broad dark vale of the Mississippi begins to roll and crumple to greet the Alleghanies. I was a Fisk student then, and all Fisk men thought that Tennessee—beyond the Veil—was theirs alone, and in vacation time they sallied forth in lusty bands to meet the county school-commissioners. Young and happy, I too went, and I shall not soon forget that summer.

First, there was a Teachers' Institute at the county-seat; and there distinguished guests of the superintendent taught the teachers fractions and spelling and other mysteries,—white teachers in the morning, Negroes at night. A picnic now and then, and a supper, and the rough world was softened by laughter and song. I remember how—but I wander.

There came a day when all the teachers left the Institute and began the hunt for schools. I learn from hearsay (for my mother was mortally afraid of firearms) that the hunting of ducks and bears and men is wonderfully interesting, but I am sure that the man who has never hunted a country school has something to learn of the pleasures of the chase. I see now the white, hot roads lazily rise and fall and wind before me under the burning July sun; I feel the deep weariness of heart and limb as ten, eight, six miles stretch relentlessly ahead; I feel my heart sink heavily as I hear again and again, "Got a teacher? Yes." So I walked on—horses were too expensive—until I wandered beyond railways, beyond stage lines, to a land of "varmints" and rattlesnakes, where the coming of a stranger was an event, and men lived and died in the shadow of one blue hill.

Sprinkled over hill and dale lay cabins and farmhouses, shut out from the world by the forests and the rolling hills toward the east. There I found at last a little school. Josie told me of it; she was a thin, homely girl of twenty, with a dark-brown face and thick, hard hair. I had crossed the stream at Watertown, and rested under the great willows; then I had gone to the little cabin in the lot where Josie was resting on her way to town. The gaunt farmer made me welcome, and Josie, hearing my errand, told me anxiously that they wanted a school over the hill; that but once since the war had a teacher been there; that she herself longed to learn,—and thus she ran on, talking fast and loud, with much earnestness and energy.

Next morning I crossed the tall round hill, lingered to look at the blue and yellow mountains stretching toward the Carolinas, then plunged into the wood, and came out at Josie's home. It was a dull frame cottage with four rooms, perched just below the brow of the hill, amid peach trees. The father was a quiet, simple soul, calmly ignorant, with no touch of vulgarity. The mother was different,—strong, bustling, and energetic, with a quick, restless tongue, and an ambition to live "like folks."

There was a crowd of children. Two boys had gone away. There remained two growing girls; a shy midget of eight; John, tall, awkward, and eighteen; Jim, younger, quicker, and better looking; and two babies of indefinite age. Then there was Josie herself. She seemed to be the center of the family: always busy at service, or at home, or berry-picking; a little nervous and inclined to scold, like her mother, yet faithful, too, like her father. She had about her a certain fineness, the shadow of an unconscious moral heroism that would willingly give all of life to make life broader, deeper, and fuller for her and hers.

I saw much of this family afterwards, and grew to love them for their honest efforts to be decent and comfortable, and for their knowledge of their own ignorance. There was with them no affectation. The mother would scold the father for being so "easy"; Josie would roundly berate the boys for carelessness; and all know that it was a hard thing to dig a living out of a rocky side-hill.

I secured the school. I remember the day I rode horseback out to the commissioner's house with a pleasant young white fellow who wanted the white school. The road ran down the bed of a stream; the sun laughed and the water jingled, and we rode on. "Come in," said the commissioner,— "come in. Have a seat. Yes, that certificate will do. Stay to dinner. What do you want a month?" "Oh," thought I, "this is lucky"; but even then fell the first awful shadow of the Veil, for they ate first, then I—alone.

The schoolhouse was a log hut, where Colonel Wheeler used to shelter his corn. It sat in a lot behind a rail fence and thorn bushes, near the sweetest of springs. There was an entrance where a door once was, and within, a massive rickety fireplace; great chinks between the logs served as windows. Furniture was scarce. A pale blackboard crouched in the corner. My desk was made of three boards, reinforced at critical points, and my chair, borrowed from the landlady, had to be returned every night. Seats for the children—these puzzled me much. I was haunted by a New England vision of neat little desks and chairs, but, alas! the reality was rough plank benches without backs, and at times without legs. They had the one virtue of making naps dangerous,— possibly fatal, for the floor was not to be trusted.

It was a hot morning late in July when the school opened. I trembled when I heard the patter of little feet down the dusty road, and saw the growing row of dark solemn faces and bright eager eyes facing me. First came Josie and her brothers and sisters. The longing to know, to be a student in the great school at Nashville, hovered like a star above this child-woman amid her work and worry, and she studied doggedly. There were the Dowells from their farm over toward Alexandria,—Fanny, with her smooth black face and wondering eyes; Martha, brown and dull; the pretty girl-wife of a brother, and the younger brood.

There were the Burkes,—two brown and yellow lads, and a tiny haughty-eyed girl. Fat Reuben's little chubby girl came, with golden face and old-gold hair, faithful and solemn. 'Thenie was on hand early,—a jolly, ugly, good-hearted girl, who slyly dipped snuff and looked after her little bow-legged brother. When her mother could spare her, 'Tildy came,—a midnight beauty, with starry eyes and tapering limbs; and her brother, correspondingly homely. And then the big boys,—the hulking Lawrences; the lazy Neills, unfathered sons of mother and daughter; Hickman, with a stoop in his shoulders; and the rest.

There they sat, nearly thirty of them, on the rough benches, their faces shading from a pale cream to a deep brown, the little feet bare and swinging, the eyes full of expectation, with here and there a twinkle of mischief, and the hands grasping Webster's blue-back spelling-book. I loved my school, and the fine faith the children had in the wisdom of their teacher was truly marvelous. We read and spelled together, wrote a little, picked flowers, sang, and listened to stories of the world beyond the hill.

At times the school would dwindle away, and I would start out. I would visit Mun Eddings, who lived in two very dirty rooms, and ask why little Lugene, whose flaming face seemed ever ablaze with the dark-red hair uncombed, was absent all last week, or why I missed so often the inimitable rags of Mack and Ed. Then the father, who worked Colonel Wheeler's farm on shares, would tell me how the crops needed the boys; and the thin, slovenly mother, whose face was pretty when washed, assured me that Lugene must mind the baby. "But we'll start them again next week." When the Lawrences stopped, I knew that the doubts of the old folks about book-learning had conquered again, and so, toiling up the hill, and getting as far into the cabin as possible, I put Cicero "pro Archia Poeta" into the simplest English with local applications, and usually convinced them—for a week or so.

On Friday nights I often went home with some of the children,—sometimes to Doc Burke's farm. He was a great, loud, thin Black, ever working, and trying to buy the seventy-five acres of hill and dale where he lived; but people said that he would surely fail, and the "white folks would get it all." His wife was a magnificent Amazon, with saffron face and shining hair, uncorseted and barefooted, and the children were strong and beautiful. They lived in a one-and-a-half-room cabin in the hollow of the farm, near the spring. The front room was full of great fat white beds, scrupulously neat; and there were bad chromos on the walls, and a tired center-table. In the tiny back kitchen

I was often invited to "take out and help" myself to fried chicken and wheat biscuit, "meat" and corn pone, string-beans and berries.

At first I used to be a little alarmed at the approach of bedtime in the lone bedroom, but embarrassment was very deftly avoided. First, all the children nodded and slept, and were stowed away in one great pile of goose feathers; next, the mother and the father discreetly slipped away to the kitchen while I went to bed; then, blowing out the dim light, they retired in the dark. In the morning all were up and away before I thought of awaking. Across the road, where fat Reuben lived, they all went out-doors while the teacher retired, because they did not boast the luxury of a kitchen.

I liked to stay with the Dowells, for they had four rooms and plenty of good country fare. Uncle Bird had a small, rough farm, all woods and hills, miles from the big road; but he was full of tales,—he preached now and then,— and with his children, berries, horses, and wheat he was happy and prosperous. Often, to keep the peace, I must go where life was less lovely; for instance, 'Tildy's mother was incorrigibly dirty, Reuben's larder was limited seriously, and herds of untamed insects wandered over the Eddingses' beds. Best of all I loved to go to Josie's, and sit on the porch, eating peaches, while the mother bustled and talked: how Josie had bought the sewing-machine; how Josie worked at service in winter, but that four dollars a month was "mighty little" wages; how Josie longed to go away to school, but that it "looked like" they never could get far enough ahead to let her; how the crops failed and the well was yet unfinished; and, finally, how "mean" some of the white folks were.

For two summers I lived in this little world; it was dull and humdrum. The girls looked at the hill in wistful longing, and the boys fretted and haunted Alexandria. Alexandria was "town,"—a straggling, lay village of houses, churches, and shops, and an aristocracy of Toms, Dicks, and Captains. Cuddled on the hill to the north was the village of the colored folks, who lived in three- or four-room unpainted cottages, some neat and homelike, and some dirty. The dwellings were scattered rather aimlessly, but they centered about the twin temples of the hamlet, the Methodist and the Hard-Shell Baptist churches. These, in turn, leaned gingerly on a sad-colored schoolhouse. Hither my little world wended its crooked way on Sunday to meet other worlds, and gossip, and wonder, and make the weekly sacrifice with frenzied priest at the altar of the "old-time religion." Then the soft melody and mighty cadences of Negro song fluttered and thundered.

I have called my tiny community a world, and so its isolation made it; and yet there was among us but a half-awakened common consciousness, sprung from common joy and grief, at burial, birth, or wedding; from a common hardship in poverty, poor land, and low wages; and above all, from the sight of the Veil that hung between us and Opportunity. All this caused us to think some thoughts together; but these, when ripe for speech, were spoken in various languages. Those whose eyes twenty-five or more years before had seen "the glory of the coming of the Lord," saw in every present hindrance or help a dark fatalism bound to bring all things right in His own good time. The mass of those to whom slavery was a dim recollection of childhood found the world a puzzling thing: it asked little of them, and they answered with little, and yet it ridiculed their offering. Such a paradox they could not understand, and therefore sank into listless indifference, or shiftlessness, or reckless bravado. There were, however, some—such as Josie, Jim and Ben— to whom War, Hell, and Slavery were but childhood tales, whose young appetites had been whetted to an edge by school and story and half-awakened thought. Ill could they be content, born without and beyond the World. And their weak wings beat against their barriers,—barriers of caste, of youth, of life; at last, in dangerous moments, against everything that opposed even a whim.

ERE SLEEP COMES DOWN TO SOOTHE THE WEARY EYES

PAUL LAURENCE DUNBAR

Ere sleep comes down to soothe the weary eyes,
Which all the day with ceaseless care have sought
The magic gold which from the seeker flies;
Ere dreams put on the gown and cap of thought,
And make the waking world a world of lies,—
Of lies most palpable, uncouth, forlorn,
That say life's full of aches and tears and sighs,—
Oh, how with more than dreams the soul is torn,
Ere sleep comes down to soothe the weary eyes.

Ere sleep comes down to soothe the weary eyes,
Now all the griefs and heartaches we have known
Come up like pois'nous vapors that arise
From some base witch's caldron, when the crone,
To work some potent spell, her magic plies.
The past which held its share of bitter pain,
Whose ghost we prayed that Time might exorcise,
Comes up, is lived and suffered o'er again,
Ere sleep comes down to soothe the weary eyes.

Ere sleep comes down to soothe the weary eyes,
What phantoms fill the dimly lighted room;
What ghostly shades in awe-creating guise
Are bodied forth within the teeming gloom.
What echoes great of sad and soul-sick cries,
And pangs of vague inexplicable pain
That pay the spirit's ceaseless enterprise,
Come thronging through the chambers of the brain,
Ere sleep comes down to soothe the weary eyes.

Ere sleep comes down to soothe the weary eyes,
Where ranges forth the spirit far and free?
Through what strange realms and unfamiliar skies
Tends her far course to lands of mystery?
To lands unspeakable—beyond surmise,
Where shapes unknowable to being spring,
Till, faint of wing, the Fancy fails and dies

Much wearied with the spirit's journeying,
Ere sleep comes down to soothe the weary eyes.

Ere sleep comes down to soothe the weary eyes,
Now questioneth the soul that other soul—
The inner sense which neither cheats nor lies,
But self exposes unto self, a scroll
Full writ with all life's acts unwise or wise,
In characters indelible and known;
So, trembling with the shock of sad surprise,
The soul doth view its awful self alone,
Ere sleep comes down to soothe the weary eyes.

When sleep comes down to seal the weary eyes,
The last dear sleep whose soft embrace is balm,
And whom sad sorrow teaches us to prize
For kissing all our passions into calm,
Ah, then, no more we heed the sad world's cries,
Or seek to probe th' eternal mystery,
Or fret our souls at long-withheld replies,
At glooms through which our visions cannot see,
When sleep comes down to seal the weary eyes.

THE LAND OF LAUGHTER

ANGELINA W. GRIMKE

Once upon a time there were two dear little boys, and they were all alone in the world. They lived with a cruel old man and old woman, who made them work hard, very hard—all day, and beat them when they did not move fast enough, and always, every night, before they went to bed. They slept in an attic on a rickety, narrow bed, that went screech! screech! whenever they moved. And, in the summer, they nearly died with the heat up there; and in the winter with the cold.

One wintry night, when they were both weeping very bitterly after a particularly hard beating, they suddenly heard a pleasant voice saying:

"Why are you crying, little boys?"

They looked up, and there in the moonlight, by their bed, was the dearest little old lady. She was dressed all in grey, from the peak of her little pointed hat to her little, buckled shoes. She held a black cane much taller than her little self. Her hair fell about her ears in tiny, grey corkscrew curls; and they bobbed about as she moved. Her eyes were black and bright—as bright as— well, as that lovely, white light in the fire. And her cheeks were as red as an apple.

"Why are you crying, little boys?" she asked again, in a lovely, low, little voice.

"Because we are tired and sore and hungry and cold; and we are all alone in the world; and we don't know how to laugh any more. We should so like to laugh again."

"Why, that's easy," she said, "it's just like this," and she laughed a little, joyous, musical laugh. "Try!" she commanded.

They tried, but their laughing boxes were very rusty and they made horrid sounds.

"Well," she said, "I advise you to pack up, and go away, as soon as you can, to the Land of Laughter. You'll soon learn there, I can tell you."

"Is there such a land?" they asked doubtfully.

"To be sure there is," she answered, the least bit sharply.

"We never heard of it," they said.

"Well, I'm sure there must be plenty of things you never heard about," she said just the "leastest" bit more sharply. "In a moment you'll be telling me the flowers don't talk together, and the birds."

"We never heard of such a thing," they said in surprise, their eyes like saucers.

"There!" she said, bobbing her little curls. "What did I tell you. You have much to learn."

"How do you get to the Land of Laughter?" they asked.

"You go out of the eastern gate of the town, just as the sun is rising; and you take the highway there, and follow it; and if you go with it long enough, it will bring you to the gate of the Land of Laughter. It is a long, long way from here; and it will take you many days."

The words had scarcely left her mouth when, lo! the little lady disappeared, and where she had stood was the white square of moonlight—nothing else.

And without more ado these two little boys put their arms round each other, and fell fast asleep. And in the grey, just before daybreak, they awoke and dressed; and putting on their little ragged caps and mittens, for it was a wintry day, they stole out of the house, and made for the eastern gate. And just as they reached it and passed through, the whole east leapt into fire.

The Land of Laughter

All day they walked, and many days thereafter; and kindly people, by the way, took them in and gave them food and drink and sometimes a bed at night. Often they slept by the roadside; but they didn't mind that for the climate was delightful—not too hot, and not too cold. They soon threw away their ragged little mittens.

They walked for many days; and there was no Land of Laughter. Once they met an old man, richly dressed, with shining jewels on his fingers, and he stopped them and asked:

"Where are you going so fast, little boys?"

"We are going to the Land of Laughter," they said very gravely.

"That," said the old man, "is a very foolish thing to do. Come with me and I will take you to the Land of Riches. I will cover you with beautiful garments, and give you jewels and a castle to live in with servants and horses and many things besides."

And they said to him, "No, we wish to learn how to laugh again; we have forgotten how, and we are going to the Land of Laughter."

"You will regret not going with me. See if you don't," he said, and he left them in quite a huff.

And they walked again, many days, and again they met an old man. He was tall and imposing-looking and very dignified. And he said:

"Where are you going so fast, little boys?"

"We are going to the Land of Laughter," they said together very seriously.

"What!" he said, "that is an extremely foolish thing to do. Come with me, and I will give you power. I will make you great men; generals, kings, emperors. Whatever you desire to accomplish will be permitted you."

And they said politely:

"Thank you, very much, but we have forgotten how to laugh; and we are going there to learn how."

He looked upon them haughtily, without speaking, and disappeared.

And they walked and walked more days; and they met another old man. And he was clad in rags; and his face was thin; and his eyes were unhappy. And he whispered to them:

"Where are you going so fast, little boys?"

"We are going to the Land of Laughter," they answered, without a smile.

"Laughter! laughter! that is useless. Come with me and I will show you the beauty of life through sacrifice, suffering for others. That is the only life. I come from the Land of Sacrifice."

And they thanked him kindly, but said:

"We have suffered enough. We have forgotten how to laugh. We would learn again." And they went on; and he looked after them wistfully.

They walked more days; and at last they came to the Land of Laughter. And how do you suppose they knew this? Because they could hear, over the wall, the sound of joyous laughter—the laughter of men, women and little children.

And one sat guarding the gate, and they went to her.

"We have come a long, long distance; and we would enter the Land of Laughter."

"Let me see you smile, first," she said gently. "I sit at the gate and no one who does not know how to smile may enter into the Land of Laughter."

And they tried to smile, but could not.

"Go away and practise," she said kindly, "and come back tomorrow."

And they went away, and practised all night how to smile; and, in the morning, they returned. And the gentle lady at the gate said:

"Dear little boys, have you learned how to smile?"

And they said: "We have tried. How is this?"

"Better," she said, "much better. Practise some more, and come back tomorrow."

And they went away obediently and practised.

And they came the third day. And she said:

"Now, try again."

And tears of delight came into her lovely eyes.

"Those were very beautiful smiles," she said. "Now you may enter."

And she unlocked the gate and kissed them both, and they entered the beautiful Land of Laughter.

Never had they seen such blue skies, such green trees and grass; never had they heard such bird song.

And people, men, women and children, laughing softly, came to meet them, and took them in, and made them at home; and soon, very soon, they learned to laugh. All day they laughed, and even in their sleep. And they grew up here, and married, and had laughing, happy children. And sometimes they thought of the Land of Riches, and said, "Ah! well"; and sometimes of the Land of Power, and sighed a little; and sometimes of the Land of Sacrifice—and their eyes were wistful. But they soon forgot, and laughed again. And they grew old, laughing. And when they died—a laugh was on their lips. Thus are things in the beautiful Land of Laughter.

THE WEB OF CIRCUMSTANCE

CHARLES W. CHESNUTT

Some time, we are told, when the cycle of years has rolled around, there is to be another golden age, when all men will dwell together in love and harmony, and when peace and righteousness shall prevail for a thousand years. God speed the day, and let not the shining thread of hope become so enmeshed in the web of circumstance that we lose sight of it; but give us here and there, and now and then, some little foretaste of this golden age, that we may the more patiently and hopefully await its coming!

IS THE GAME WORTH THE CANDLE?

JAMES E. SHEPARD

A man's life depends upon his emotions, his aspirations, his determinations.

A young man, somebody's son, starts out with the determination that the world is indebted to him for a good time. "Dollars were made to spend. I am young, and every man must sow his wild oats and then settle down. I want to be a 'hail fellow well met' with every one."

With this determination uppermost in his life purpose he starts out to be a good-timer. Perhaps some mother expects to hear great things of her boy, some father's hopes are centered in him, but what does that matter? "I am a good-timer." From one gayety to another, from one glass to another, from one sin to another, and the good-timer at last is broken in health, deserted by friends, and left alone to die. Thus the "man about town" passes off the stage. When you ask some of his friends about him, the answer is, "Oh, John was all right, but he lived too fast. I like good times as well as anyone, but I could not keep up with John." Was the game worth the candle?

Two pictures came before my mind: two cousins, both of them young men. One started out early in life with the determination of getting along "easy," shirking work, and looking for a soft snap. His motto was, "The world owes me a living, and I am going to get mine." He was employed first by one firm and then by another; if anything that he considered hard came along, he would pay another fellow to do the work and he "took things easy." It was not long before no one would hire him. He continued to hold the idea that the world was indebted to him and furthermore, he arrogated a belief that what another man had accumulated he could borrow without his knowledge. He forged another man's name, was detected, and sentenced to the penitentiary and is now wearing the badge of felony and shame—the convict's stripes. Is the game worth the candle?

The other cousin started out with a determination altogether different. He believed with Lord Brougham, that if he were a bootblack he would strive to be the best bootblack in England. He began in a store as a window-cleaner, and washed windows so well that they sparkled like diamonds under the sun. As a clerk, no customer was too insignificant to be greeted with a smile or pleasant word; no task was too great for him to attempt. Thus step by step, he advanced, each day bringing new duties and difficulties but each day also bringing new strength and determination to master them, and today that cousin is a man of wealth and an honored citizen, blessed, too, with a happy home.

Some young men start life with the idea that every dollar made requires that one dollar and a half shall be spent; in order to be noticed they must make a big show, give big dinners, carriage drives, and parties, invite friends to the theaters, and have a "swell" time; must do like Mr. "So-and-So." They forget in their desire to copy, that Mr. "So-and-So," their pattern, has already made his fortune; that he began to save before he began to spend. But no, his name appears often in the papers and they think also that theirs must. So they begin their careers. A few years pass. The young men marry; their debts begin to accumulate and to press them, their countenances are always woe-begone; where once were smiles, now are frowns, and the homes are pictures of gloom and shadows. The lesson is plain.

Debt is the greatest burden that can be put upon man; it makes him afraid to look honest men in the face. No man can be a leader in the fullest sense who is burdened by a great debt. If there is any young man who is spending more than he is making, let him ask himself the question, Is the game worth the candle?

I know another young man who believed he could be happy by spending one-third of what he made and saving the other portion. He said to me, "some day I want to marry and I want to treat my wife better, if possible, than she was treated at home. I want to respect my fellow man, I want to be a leader, and I know I can only do so by saving a part of what I make." It was my good pleasure, a few weeks ago, to visit the city where this young man is practising medicine. He carried me over that town in an automobile, he entertained me in his $5000 home, he showed me other property which he owned. Ah, his indeed was a happy home. Life to him was blessedly real.

A young man starts out in life with the determination to fight his way by physical force to the front ranks. Bruised, disfigured, or killed, he is forced back even beyond the lines again. A religiously inclined youth asked his pastor, "Do you think it would be wrong for me to learn the noble art of self-defense?" "Certainly not," replied the pastor, "I learned it in youth myself, and I have found it of great value in my life." "Indeed, sir, did you learn the Old English system or the Sullivan system" "Neither; I learned Solomon's system!" replied the minister. "Yes, you will find it laid down in the first verse of the fifteenth chapter of Proverbs, 'A soft answer turneth away wrath'; it is the best system of self-defense I know."

Another young man starts life with a wrong idea regarding city and country life. Born in the country he is free, his thoughts and ambitions can feed on a pure atmosphere, but he thinks his conditions and his surroundings are circumscribed; he longs for the city, with its bigness, its turmoil, and its conflicts. He leaves the old homestead, the quiet village, the country people, and hies himself to the city. He forgets to a large extent the good boy he used to be, in the desire to keep up with the fashions and to make the people forget that he was once a country boy. City life, as is often the case, breaks up his youth, destroys his morals, undermines his character, steals his reputation, and finally leaves the promising youth a wrecked man. Was the game worth the candle?

Young men, never be ashamed of the old log-cabin in the country, or the old bonnet your mother used to wear, or the jean pants your father used to toil in. I had rather be a poor country boy with limited surroundings and a pure heart than to be a city man bedecked in the latest fashions and weighted down with money, having no morals, no character. I had rather have the religion and faith of my fathers than to have the highest offices. I had rather have glorious life, pure and lofty, than to have great riches. Sir Walter Scott was right when he said:

"Sound, sound the clarion, fill the fife,
To all the sensual world proclaim:
One crowded hour of glorious life
Is worth an age without a name."

There are two old Dutch words which have resounded through the world, "*Neen nimmer*," "No, never." The fleets of Spain heard it, and understood it fully, when they saw the sinking Dutch ships with the flags nailed to the shattered mainmast, crying, "*Neen nimmer*," which indicated that they would never surrender.

Will the young men who are to be the leaders, spend their hours in riotous living? No, never! Will they be false to duty? No, never! Will they shirk? No, never! Will they be disloyal to self, to home, to country, and to God? No, never!

Croesus was a rich man, a king. One day Croesus said to Solon, the philosopher, "Do you not think I am a happy man?" Solon answered, "Alas, I do not know, Croesus; that life is happy that ends well." A few years later when Croesus had lost his wealth, his kingdom, and his health, and had been deserted by those who in his days of glory ran to do his slightest bidding, Croesus in anguish and misery exclaimed, "Solon, Solon, thou saidst truly that life is well and happy that ends well."

O BLACK AND UNKNOWN BARDS

JAMES WELDON JOHNSON

O black and unknown bards of long ago,
How came your lips to touch the sacred fire?
How, in your darkness, did you come to know
The power and beauty of the minstrel's lyre?
Who first from midst his bonds lifted his eyes?
Who first from out the still watch, lone and long,
Feeling the ancient faith of prophets rise
Within his dark-kept soul, burst into song?

Heart of what slave poured out such melody
As "Steal away to Jesus"? On its strains
His spirit must have nightly floated free,
Though still about his hands he felt his chains.
Who heard great "Jordan roll"? Whose starward eye
Saw chariot "swing low"? And who was he
That breathed that comforting, melodic sigh,
"Nobody knows de trouble I see?"

What merely living clod, what captive thing,
Could up toward God through all its darkness grope,
And find within its deadened heart to sing
These songs of sorrow, love, and faith, and hope?
How did it catch that subtle undertone,
That note in music heard not with the ears?
How sound the elusive reed so seldom blown,
Which stirs the soul or melts the heart to tears.

Not that great German master in his dream
Of harmonies that thundered 'mongst the stars
At the creation, ever heard a theme
Nobler than "Go down, Moses." Mark its bars,
How like a mighty trumpet-call they stir
The blood. Such are the notes that men have sung
Going to valorous deeds; such tones there were
That helped make history when Time was young.

There is a wide, wide wonder in it all,
That from degraded rest and servile toil
The fiery spirit of the seer should call

These simple children of the sun and soil.
O black slave singers, gone, forgot, unfamed,
You—you alone, of all the long, long line
Of those who've sung untaught, unknown, unnamed,
Have stretched out upward, seeking the divine.

You sang not deeds of heroes or of kings;
No chant of bloody war, no exulting pean
Of arms-won triumphs; but your humble strings
You touched in chord with music empyrean.
You sang far better than you knew; the songs
That for your listeners' hungry hearts sufficed
Still live,—but more than this to you belongs:
You sang a race from wood and stone to Christ.

THE GREATEST MENACE OF THE SOUTH

WILLIAM J. EDWARDS

In every age there are great and pressing problems to be solved. Perhaps no section of this country has been confronted with more difficult problems than the South. I therefore wish to present what I consider to be the greatest menace of this section.

The one thing to-day, in which we stand in greatest danger, is the loss of the fertility of the soil. If we should lose this, as we are gradually doing, then all is lost. If we should save it, then all other things will be added. Our great need is the conservation and preservation of the soil.

The increased crops which we have in the South occasionally, are not due to improved methods of farming, but to increased acreage. Thousands of acres of new land are added each year and our increase in farm production is due to the strength of these fresh lands. There is not much more woodland to be taken in as new farm lands, for this source has been well nigh exhausted. We must then, within a few years, expect a gradual reduction in the farm production of the South.

Already the old farm lands that have been in cultivation for the past fifty or fifty-five years are practically worn out. I have seen in my day where forty acres of land twenty or twenty-five years ago would produce from twenty to twenty-five bales of cotton each year, and from 800 to 1000 bushels of corn. Now, these forty acres will not produce more than eight or nine bales of cotton and hardly enough corn to feed two horses. In fact, one small family cannot obtain a decent support from the land which twenty years ago supported three families in abundance. This farm is not on the hillside, neither has it been worn away by erosion. It is situated in the lowlands, in the black prairie, and is considered the best farm on a large plantation. This condition obtains in all parts of the South today. This constant deterioration of land, this gradual reduction of crops year after year, if kept up for the next fifty years, will surely prove disastrous to the South.

Practically all the land in the black belt of the South is cultivated by Negroes and the farm production has decreased so rapidly during the last ten or fifteen years that the average Negro farmer hardly makes sufficient to pay his rent and buy the few necessaries of life.

Of course, here and there where a tenant has been lucky enough to get hold of some new land, he makes a good crop, but after three or four years of cultivation, his crop begins to decrease and this decrease is kept up as long as he keeps the land. Instead of improving, the tenant's condition becomes worse each year until he finds it impossible to support his family on the farm.

Farm after farm is being abandoned or given up to the care of the old men and women. Already, most of these are too old and feeble to do effective work.

Now, the chief cause of these farms becoming less productive is the failure on the part of the farmers to add something to the land after they have gathered their crops. They seem to think that the land contains an inexhaustible supply of plant food. Another cause is the failure of the farmer to rotate his crop. There are farms being cultivated in the South today where the same piece of land has been planted in cotton every year for forty or fifty years. Forty years ago, this same land would yield from one bale to one and a half per acre. And today it will take from four to six acres to produce one bale.

Still another cause for the deterioration of the soil is erosion. There is no effort put forth on the tenant's part to prevent his farm from washing away. The hillside and other rolling lands are not terraced and after being in use four or five years, practically all of these lands are washed away and as farm lands they are abandoned. Not only are the hillside lands unprotected from the beating rains and flowing streams, but the bottom or lowlands are not properly drained, and the sand washed down from the hill, the chaff and raft from previous rains soon fill the ditches and creeks and almost any ordinary rain will cause an overflow of these streams.

Under these conditions an average crop is impossible even in the best of years. At present the South does not produce one-half of the foodstuff that it consumes and if the present conditions of things continue for the next fifty years, this section of the country will be on the verge of starvation and famines will be a frequent occurrence. Of course, Negro starvation will come first, but white man starvation will surely follow. I believe, therefore, that I am justified in saying that there is even more danger in Negro starvation than there is in Negro domination.

I have noticed in this country that the sins of the races are contagious. If the Negro in a community be lazy, indifferent, and careless about his farm, the white man in the community will soon fall into the same habit. On the other hand, if the white man is smart, industrious, energetic and persevering in his general makeup, the Negro will soon fall into line; so after all, whatever helps one race in the South will help the other and whatever degrades one race in the South, sooner or later will degrade the other.

But you may reply to this assertion by saying that the Negro can go to the city and make an independent living for himself and family, but you forget that all real wealth must come from the soil and that the city cannot prosper unless the country is prosperous. When the country fails, the city feels the effect; when the country weeps, the city moans; when agriculture dies, all die. Such are the conditions which face us today. Now for the remedy.

It is worth while to remember that there are ten essential elements of plant food. If the supply of any one of the elements fails, the crop will fail. These ten elements are carbon and oxygen taken into the leaves of the plant from the air as carbon dioxide; hydrogen, a constituent of water absorbed through the plant roots; nitrogen, taken from the soil by all plants also secured from the air by legumes. The other elements are phosphorus, potassium, magnesium, calcium, iron and sulphur, all of which are secured from the soil. The soil nitrogen is contained in the organic matter or humus, and to maintain the supply of nitrogen we should keep the soil well stored with organic matter, making liberal use of clover or other legumes which have power to secure nitrogen from the inexhaustible supply in the air.

It is interesting to note that one of the ablest chemists in this country, Prof. E. W. Clark of the United States Geological Survey, has said that an acre of ground seven inches deep contains sufficient iron to produce one hundred bushels of corn every year for 200,000 years, sufficient calcium to produce one hundred bushels of corn or one bale of cotton each year for 55,000 years, enough magnesium to produce such a crop 7,000 years, enough sulphur for 10,000 years and potassium for 2,600 years, but only enough phosphorus for 130 years. The nitrogen resting upon the surface of an acre of ground is sufficient to produce one hundred bushels of corn or a bale of cotton for 700,000 years; but only enough in the plowed soil to produce fifty such crops. In other words, there are enough of eight of the elements of plant food in the ordinary soil to produce 100 bushels of corn per acre or a bale of cotton per acre for each year for 2,600 years; but only enough of the other two, phosphorus and nitrogen, to produce such crops for forty or fifty years.

Let us grant that most of our farm lands in the South have been in cultivation for fifty or seventy-five years, and in many instances for one hundred years, it is readily seen that practically all of the phosphorus and nitrogen in the plowed soil have been exhausted. Is it any wonder then that we are having such poor crops? The wonder is that our crops have kept up so well. Unless a radical change is made in our mode of farming, we must expect less and less crops each year until we have no crops, or such little that we can hardly pay the rent.

To improve and again make fertile our soils, we must restore to them the phosphorus and nitrogen which have been used up in the seventy-five or more crops that we have gathered from them. This is a herculean task but this is what confronts us and I for one believe we can accomplish it. By the proper rotation of crops, including oats, clover, cowpeas, as well as cotton and corn, and a liberal use of barnyard manure and cotton seed fertilizer, all of the necessary elements of plant food can be restored to our worn-out soil. But the proper use of these requires much painstaking study.

If the Negro is to remain the farming class in the Black Belt of the South, then he must be taught at least the rudiments of the modern methods of improving farming. He must have agricultural schools and must be encouraged to attend them. The loss of the fertility of the soil is the greatest menace of the South. How can we regain this lost fertility is the greatest question of the hour.

THE ENCHANTED SHELL

H. CORDELIA RAY

Fair, fragile Una, golden-haired,
With melancholy, dark gray eyes,
Sits on a rock by laughing waves,
Gazing into the radiant skies;

And holding to her ear a shell,
A rosy shell of wondrous form;
Quite plaintively to her it coos
Marvelous lays of sea and storm.

It whispers of a fairy home
With coral halls and pearly floors,
Where mermaids clad in glist'ning gold
Guard smilingly the jeweled doors.

She listens and her weird gray eyes
Grow weirder in their pensive gaze.
The sea birds toss her tangled curls,
The skiff lights glimmer through the haze.

Oh, strange sea-singer! what has lent
Such fascination to thy spell?
Is some celestial guardian
Prisoned within thee, tiny shell?

The Enchanted Shell

The maid sits rapt until the stars
In myriad shining clusters gleam;
"Enchanted Una," she is called
By boatmen gliding down the stream.

The tempest beats the restless seas,
The wind blows loud, fierce from the skies;
Sweet, sylph-like Una clasps the shell,
Peace brooding in her quiet eyes.

The wind blows wilder, darkness comes,
The rock is bare, night birds soar far;
Thick clouds scud o'er the gloomy heav'ns
Unvisited by any star.

Where is quaint Una? On some isle,
Dreaming 'mid music, may she be?

Or does she listen to the shell
In coral halls within the sea?

The boatmen say on stormy nights
They see rare Una with the shell,
Sitting in pensive attitude,
Is it a vision? Who can tell?

BEHIND A GEORGIA MULE

JAMES WELDON JOHNSON

Now if you wish to travel fast,
I beg you not to fool
With locomotion that's procured
Behind a Georgia mule.

When I was teaching school in the backwoods of Georgia I had, one day, to attend to some business in Mudville, an embryo city about eleven miles from my school. Now you must know that a country school teacher can do nothing without first consulting his Board of Trustees; so I notified that honorable body that there was some business of vast importance to be attended to, and asked them to meet me on Friday afternoon; they all promised to be on hand "two hours b'sun." Friday afternoon, after school was dismissed, they came in one by one until they had all gathered.

As the chairman called the meeting to order, he said: "Brederen, de objick ob dis meeting is to consider de ways ob pervidin de means ob transposin de 'fessar to Mudville." Now, by the way, the chairman of the Board was undoubtedly intended by nature for a smart man. He had a very strong weakness for using big words in the wrong place, and thought it his special duty to impress the "'fessar" at all times with his knowledge of the dictionary. Well, after much debate it was finally decided that "Brudder" Whitesides would "furnish de mule" and "Brudder Jinks de buggy" and that I should start early the next morning.

The next morning I was up quite early, because I wished to start as soon as possible in order to avoid the heat of the day. I ate breakfast and waited— six o'clock, seven o'clock, eight o'clock—and still that promised beast had not put in appearance. Knowing the proclivity of the mule to meander along as his own sweet will dictates, especially when the sun shines hot, I began to despair of reaching Mudville at all that day; but "Brudder" Jinks, with whom I boarded, seeing my melancholy state of mind, offered to hitch up Gypsy, an antiquated specimen of the mule, whose general appearance was that of the skeleton of some prehistoric animal one sees in a museum.

I accepted this proposition with haste, and repented at leisure.

I could see a weary, long-suffering look in that mule's eye, and I could imagine how his heart must have sought the vicinity of his tail, when they disturbed his dreams of green fields and pleasant pastures, and hitched him to an old buggy, to encounter the stern realities of a dusty road. "Verily, verily," I soliloquized, "the way of the mule is hard." But, putting aside all tender feelings, I jumped into the buggy and grasping a stick of quite ample proportions began to urge his muleship on his way.

Nothing of much consequence hampered our onward journey except the breaking down of three wheels and the excessive heat of the sun, which great luminary seemed not more than ninety-five miles away.

I arrived at Mudville sometime between 12 M. and 6 P. M. After having finished my business and having bountifully fed my mule on water and what grass he could nibble from around his hitching post, I bought a large watermelon and started for home. Before I was out of sight of the town, I began to have serious misgivings about reaching home before a very late hour. In the morning by various admonitions and applications of the hickory, I had been able to get my mule into a jog trot, but on the homeward journey he would not even get up a respectable walk. Well, we trudged on for two hours or more, when to my dismay he stopped,—stopped still. As the hour was getting late and it was growing dark, I began advising him—with the hickory—that it was best to proceed, but he seemed to have hardened his heart, and his back also, and paid me no heed. There I sat—all was as still as the grave, save for the dismal hoot of the screech-owl. There I was, five and a half miles from home with no prospect of getting there.

I began to coax my mule with some words which perhaps are not in the Sabbath School books, and to emphasize them with the rising and falling inflection of the stick across his back; but still he moved not. Then all at once my conscience smote me. I thought perhaps the faithful beast might be sick. My mind reverted to Balaam, whose beast spoke to him when he had smitten him but three times and here I had smitten my beast about 3,333 times. I listened almost in expectation of hearing him say, "Johnson, Johnson, why smitest thou me 3,333 times?"

I got out of the buggy and looked at the mule; he gazed at me with a sad far-away expression in his eye, which sent pangs of remorse to my heart. I thought of the cruel treatment I had given him, and on the impulse of the moment I went to the buggy, got out my large, luscious melon, burst it open and laid it on the ground before the poor animal; and I firmly resolved to be a friend of the mule ever after, and to join the Humane Society as soon as I reached Atlanta.

As I watched that mule slowly munching away at my melon, I began to wonder if I had not acted a little too hastily in giving it to him, but I smothered that thought when I remembered the pledge I had just taken. When he had finished he looked around with a satisfied air which encouraged me; so I took hold of his bridle and after stroking him gently for a moment, attempted to lead him off. But he refused to be led. He looked at me from under his shabby eyebrows, but the sad, far-away expression had vanished and in its stead there was a mischievous gleam, born of malice afore-thought. I remonstrated with him, but it only seemed to confirm his convictions that it was right for him to stand there. I thought of my melon he had just devoured; then I grew wrathy, and right there and then renounced all my Humane Society resolutions, and began to shower down on that mule torrents of abuse and hickory also, but all to no effect. Instead of advancing he began to "revance." I pulled on the bridle until my hands and arms were sore, but he only continued to back and pull me along with him. When I stopped pulling he stopped backing, and so things went on for the space of about half an hour.

I wondered what time it was. Just then the moon began to rise, from which I knew it was about 9 o'clock. My physical exertion began to tell on me and I hungered. Oh, how I hungered for a piece of that watermelon! And I hit the mule an extra blow as a result of those longings.

I was now desperate. I sat down on the side of the road and groaned; that groan came from the depths of my soul, and I know that I presented a perfect picture of despair. However, I determined to gather all my remaining strength for one final effort; so I caressed him up and down the backbone two or three times as a sort of persuader, then grasping the bridle with both hands, I began to pull, pull as I had never pulled before and as I never hope to pull again. And he began to back. I continued to pull and he continued to back.

How long this order of things might have gone on I do not know, but just then a brilliant idea struck me so forcibly as to come near knocking me down. I took the mule out, and by various tying, buckling and tangling, I hitched him up again, upside down, or wrong side out, or, well, I can't exactly explain, but anyhow when I got through his tail pointed in the direction I wanted him to go. Then I got back in the buggy and taking hold of the bridle began to pull, and he began to back; and I continued to pull, and he continued to back; and will you believe me, that mule backed all the way home! It is true we did not travel very fast but every time he would slow down, I would put a little extra force into my pull and he would put a little extra speed into his back. Ever and anon he would glance at me with that mischievous, malicious twinkle, which seemed to say "I've got you tonight," and I would smile back a quiet, self-satisfied smile and give an extra pull.

But when we got home, that mischievous, malicious twinkle changed, and he looked at me in a dazed sort of way and I smiled back quite audibly. And do you know, that mule has been in a dark brown study ever since. He is trying to get through his slow brain how I managed to make him pull me home that night.

As I jumped out of the buggy the clock struck twelve. And there at that solemn hour of the night, as the pale moon shed her silvery beams all around and as the bright stars peeped down upon me from the ethereal blue, and the gentle zephyrs wafted to me the odor of a hog-pen in the near distance, I vowed a vow, an awful vow, that so long as I breathed the vital air, never, no, never again, would I attempt to drive a Georgia mule.

HAYTI AND TOUSSAINT L'OUVERTURE

W. E. B. DUBOIS

It was in the island of Hayti that French slavery centered. Pirates from many nations, but chiefly French, began to frequent the island, and in 1663 the French annexed the eastern part, thus dividing the island between France and Spain. By 1680 there were so many slaves and mulattoes that Louis XIV issued his celebrated Code Noir, which was notable in compelling bachelor masters, fathers of slave children, to marry their concubines. Children followed the condition of the mother as to slavery or freedom; they could have no property; harsh punishments were provided for, but families could not be separated by sale except in the case of grown children; emancipation with full civil rights was made possible for any slave twenty years of age or more. When Louisiana was settled and the Alabama coast, slaves were introduced there. Louisiana was transferred to Spain in 1762, against the resistance of both settlers and slaves, but Spain took possession in 1769 and introduced more Negroes.

Later, in Hayti, a more liberal policy encouraged trade; war was over and capital and slaves poured in. Sugar, coffee, chocolate, indigo, dyes, and spices were raised. There were large numbers of mulattoes, many of whom were educated in France, and many masters married Negro women who had inherited large properties, just as in the United States to-day white men are marrying eagerly the landed Indian women in the West. When white immigration increased in 1749, however, prejudice arose against these mulattoes and severe laws were passed depriving them of civil rights, entrance into the professions, and the right to hold office; severe edicts were enforced as to clothing, names, and social intercourse. Finally, after 1777, mulattoes were forbidden to come to France.

When the French Revolution broke out, the Haytians managed to send two delegates to Paris. Nevertheless the planters maintained the upper hand, and one of the colored delegates, Oge, on returning, started a small rebellion. He and his companions were killed with great brutality. This led the French government to grant full civil rights to free Negroes. Immediately planters and free Negroes flew to arms against each other and then, suddenly, August 22, 1791, the black slaves, of whom there were four hundred and fifty-two thousand, arose in revolt to help the free Negroes.

For many years runaway slaves under their own chiefs had hidden in the mountains. One of the earliest of these chiefs was Polydor, in 1724, who was succeeded by Macandal. The great chief of these runaways or "Maroons" at the time of the slave revolt was Jean François, who was soon succeeded by Biassou.

Pierre Dominic Toussaint, known as Toussaint L'Ouverture, joined these Maroon bands, where he was called "the doctor of the armies of the king," and soon became chief aid to Jean François and Biassou. Upon their deaths Toussaint rose to the chief command. He acquired complete control over the blacks, not only in military matters, but in politics and social organization; "the soldiers regarded him as a superior being, and the farmers prostrated themselves before him. All his generals trembled before him (Dessalines did not dare to look in his face), and all the world trembled before his generals."

The revolt once started, blacks and mulattoes murdered whites without mercy and the whites retaliated. Commissioners were sent from France, who asked simply civil rights for freedmen, and not emancipation. Indeed that was all that Toussaint himself had as yet demanded. The planters intrigued with the British and this, together with the beheading of the king (an impious act in the eyes of Negroes), induced Toussaint to join the Spaniards. In 1793 British troops were landed and the French commissioners in desperation declared the slaves emancipated. This at once won back Toussaint from the Spaniards. He became supreme in the north, while Rigaud, leader of the mulattoes, held the south and the west. By 1798 the British, having lost most of their forces by yellow fever, surrendered Mole St. Nicholas to Toussaint and departed. Rigaud finally left for France, and Toussaint in 1800 was master of Hayti. He promulgated a constitution under which Hayti was to be a self-governing colony; all men were equal before the law, and trade was practically free. Toussaint was to be president for life, with the power to name his successor.

Napoleon Bonaparte, master of France, had at this time dreams of a great American empire, and replied to Toussaint's new government by sending twenty-five thousand men under his brother-in-law to subdue the presumptuous Negroes, as a preliminary step to his occupation and development of the Mississippi valley. Fierce fighting and yellow fever decimated the French, but matters went hard with the Negroes too, and Toussaint finally offered to yield. He was courteously received with military honors and then, as soon as possible, treacherously seized, bound, and sent to France. He was imprisoned at Fort Joux and died, perhaps of poison, after studied humiliations, April 7, 1803.

Thus perished the greatest of American Negroes and one of the great men of all time, at the age of fifty-six. A French planter said, "God in his terrestrial globe did not commune with a purer spirit." Wendell Phillips said, "Some doubt the courage of the Negro. Go to Hayti and stand on those fifty thousand graves of the best soldiers France ever had and ask them what they think of the Negro's sword. I would call him Napoleon, but Napoleon made his way to empire over broken oaths and through a sea of blood. This man never broke his word. I would call him Cromwell, but Cromwell was only a soldier, and the state he founded went down with him into his grave. I would call him Washington, but the great Virginian held slaves. This man risked his empire rather than permit the slave trade in the humblest village of his dominions. You think me a fanatic, for you read history, not with your eyes, but with your prejudices. But fifty years hence, when Truth gets a hearing, the Muse of history will put Phocion for the Greek, Brutus for the Roman, Hampden for the English, La Fayette for France, choose Washington as the bright consummate flower of our earlier civilization, then, dipping her pen in the sunlight, will write in the clear blue, above them all, the name of the soldier, the statesman, the martyr, Toussaint L'Ouverture."

The treacherous killing of Toussaint did not conquer Hayti. In 1802 and 1803 some forty thousand French soldiers died of war and fever. A new colored leader, Dessalines, arose and all the eight thousand remaining French surrendered to the blockading British fleet.

The effect of all this was far-reaching. Napoleon gave up his dream of American empire and sold Louisiana for a song. "Thus, all of Indian Territory, all of Kansas and Nebraska and Iowa and Wyoming and Montana and the Dakotas, and most of Colorado and Minnesota, and all of Washington and Oregon states, came to us as the indirect work of a despised Negro. Praise, if you will, the work of a Robert Livingstone or a Jefferson, but to-day let us not forget our debt to Toussaint L'Ouverture, who was indirectly the means of America's expansion by the Louisiana Purchase of 1803."

HIS MOTTO

LOTTIE BURRELL DIXON ·

"But I can't leave my business affairs and go off on a fishing trip now."

The friend and specialist who had tricked John Durmont into a confession of physical bankruptcy, and made him submit to an examination in spite of himself, now sat back with an "I wash my hands of you" gesture.

"Very well, you can either go to Maine, now, at once, or you'll go to—well, as I'm only your spiritual adviser, my prognostications as to your ultimate destination would probably have very little weight with you."

"Oh, well, if you are so sure, I suppose I can cut loose now, if it comes to a choice like that."

The doctor smiled his satisfaction. "So you prefer to bear the ills of New York than to fly to others you know not of, eh?"

"Oh, have a little mercy on Shakespeare, at least. I'll go."

And thus it was that a week later found Durmont as deep in the Maine woods as he could get and still be within reach of a telegraph wire. And much to his surprise he found he liked it.

As he lay stretched at full length on the soft turf, the breath of the pines filled his lungs, the lure of the lake made him eager to get to his fishing tackle, and he admitted to himself that a man needed just such a holiday as this in order to keep his mental and physical balance.

Returning to the gaily painted frame building, called by courtesy the "Hotel," which nestled among the pines, he met the youthful operator from the near-by station looking for him with a message from his broker. A complicated situation had arisen in Amalgamated Copper, and an immediate answer was needed. Durmont had heavy investments in copper, though his business was the manufacture of electrical instruments.

He walked back to the office with the operator while pondering the answer, then having written it, handed it to the operator saying, "Tell them to rush answer."

The tall lank youth, whose every movement was a protest against being hurried, dragged himself over to the telegraph key.

"'S open."

"What's open?"

"Wire."

"Well, is that the only wire you have?"

"Yep."

"What in the world am I going to do about this message?"

"Dunno, maybe it will close bime-by." And the young lightning slinger pulled towards him a lurid tale of the Wild West, and proceeded to enjoy himself.

"And meanwhile, what do you suppose is going to happen to me?" thundered Durmont. "Haven't you ambition enough to look around your wire and see if you can find the trouble?"

"Lineman's paid to look up trouble; I'm not," was the surly answer.

Durmont was furious, but what he was about to say was cut off by a quiet voice at his elbow.

"I noticed linemen repairing wires upon the main road, that's where this wire is open. If you have any message you are in a hurry to send, perhaps I can help you out."

Durmont turned to see a colored boy of fifteen whose entrance he had not noticed.

"What can you do about it?" he asked contemptuously, "take it into town in an ox team?"

"I can send it by wireless, if that is sufficiently quick."

Durmont turned to the operator at the table.

"Is there a wireless near here?"

"He owns one, you'll have to do business with him on that," said the youth with a grin at Durmont's unconcealed prejudice.

It would be hard to estimate the exact amount of respect, mingled with surprise, with which the city man now looked at the boy whose information he had evidently doubted till confirmed by the white boy.

"Suppose you've got some kind of tom-fool contraption that will take half a day to get a message into the next village. Here I stand to lose several thousands because this blame company runs only one wire down to this camp. Where is this apparatus of yours? Might as well look at it while I'm waiting for this one-wire office to get into commission again."

"It's right up on top of the hill," answered the colored boy. "Here, George, I brought down this wireless book if you want to look it over, it's better worth reading than that stuff you have there," and tossing a book on the table he went out, followed by Durmont.

A couple of minutes' walk brought them in sight of the sixty-foot aerial erected on the top of a small shack.

"Not much to look at, but I made it all myself."

HIS MOTTO

"How did you happen to construct this?" And Durmont really tried to keep the emphasis off the "you."

"Well, I'm interested in all kinds of electrical experiments, and have kept up reading and studying ever since I left school, then when I came out here on my uncle's farm, he let me rig up this wireless, and I can talk to a chum of mine down in the city. And when I saw the wire at the station was gone up, I thought I might possibly get your message to New York through him."

They had entered the one-room shack which contained a long table holding a wireless outfit, a couple of chairs and a shelf of books. On the walls were tacked pictures of aviators and drawings of aeroplanes. A three-foot model of a biplane hung in a corner.

"Now if he is only in," said the boy, going over to the table and giving the call.

"He's there," he said eagerly, holding out his hand for the message.

Durmont handed it to him. His face still held the look of doubt and unbelief as he looked at the crude, home-made instruments.

"Suppose I might as well have hired a horse and taken it into town." But the sputtering wire drowned his voice.

"And get on your wheel and go like blazes. Tell 'em to rush answer. This guy here thinks a colored boy is only an animated shoe-blacking outfit; it's up to us to remedy that defect in his education, see!" Thus sang the wires as Durmont paced the floor.

"I said," began the nervous man as the wires became quiet. "I—" again the wire sputtered, and he couldn't hear himself talk. When it was quiet, he tried again, but as soon as he began to grumble, the wire began to sputter. He glanced suspiciously at the boy, but the latter was earnestly watching his instruments.

"Say," shouted Durmont, "does that thing have to keep up that confounded racket all the time?"

"I had to give him some instructions, you know, and also keep in adjustment."

"Well, I'll get out of adjustment myself if that keeps up."

Durmont resigned himself to silence, and strangely enough, so did the wire. Walking around the room he noticed over the shelf of books a large white sheet on which was printed in gilt letters:

"I WILL STUDY AND MAKE READY, AND MAYBE MY CHANCE WILL COME."

—ABRAHAM LINCOLN.

Durmont read this, and then looked at the boy as if seeing him for the first time. Again he looked at the words, and far beyond them he saw his own struggling boyhood, climbing daily Life's slippery path, trying to find some hold by which to pull himself up. And as he watched the brown-skinned boy bending over the instruments, instinct told him here was one who would find it still harder to fight his way up, because of caste.

"Ah!"

The exclamation startled him. The boy with phones adjusted was busily writing.

"Well, has that partner of yours got that message down at his end yet?"

"Yes, sir, and here is your answer from New York."

"Why it's only been half an hour since I wrote it," said Durmont.

"Yes, that horse wouldn't have got into town yet," grinned the boy.

Durmont snatched the paper, read it, threw his cap in the air, exclaiming, "The day is saved. Boy, you're a winner. How much?" putting his hand in his pocket suggestively.

"How much you owe to my help, I don't know," answered the lad sagely. "I offered to help you because you needed it, and I was glad of the chance to prove what I believed I could do. I'm satisfied because I succeeded."

Durmont sat down heavily on the other chair; his nerves couldn't stand much more in one afternoon. To find himself threatened with a large financial loss; to have this averted by the help of the scientific knowledge of a colored boy, and that boy rating the fact of his success higher than any pecuniary compensation—he had to pull himself together a bit.

His eyes fell on the motto on the wall. He read it thoughtfully, considered how hard the boy had worked because of that, his hopes of the future based on that; saw the human element in him as it had not appealed to him before, and then turning something over in his mind, muttered to himself, "It's nobody's business if I do."

He got up, and walking over to the boy said: "What's your name?"

"Robert Hilton."

"Well, Robert, that motto you've got up there is a pretty good one to tie to. You certainly have studied; you have made yourself ready as far as your resources will permit, and I'll be hanged if I don't stand for the 'chance.' In the manufacturing of electrical instruments you could have great opportunity for inventive talent, and in my concern you shall have your chance, and go as far as your efficiency will carry you. What do you say, would you care for it?"

"I'd care for it more than any other thing on earth, and am very grateful for the chance."

"The chance wouldn't be standing here now if you had not had the inclination and the determination to live up to those words on the wall."

THE MONTHS

H. CORDELIA RAY

January

To herald in another year,
With rhythmic note the snowflakes fall
Silently from their crystal courts,
To answer Winter's call.
Wake, mortal! Time is winged anew!
Call Love and Hope and Faith to fill
The chambers of thy soul to-day;
Life hath its blessings still!

February

The icicles upon the pane
Are busy architects; they leave
What temples and what chiseled forms
Of leaf and flower! Then believe
That though the woods be brown and bare,
And sunbeams peep through cloudy veils,
Though tempests howl through leaden skies,
The springtime never fails!

March

Robin! Robin! call the Springtime
!March is halting on his way;
Hear the gusts. What! snowflakes falling!
Look not for the grass to-day.
Ay, the wind will frisk and play,
And we cannot say it nay.

April

She trips across the meadows,
The weird, capricious elf!
The buds unfold their perfumed cups
For love of her sweet self;
And silver-throated birds begin to tune their lyres,
While wind-harps lend their strains to Nature's magic choirs.

May

Sweet, winsome May, coy, pensive fay,
Comes garlanded with lily-beds,
And apple blooms shed incense through the bow'r,
To be her dow'r;
While through the deafy dells
A wondrous concert swells
To welcome May, the dainty fay.

June

Roses, roses, roses,
Creamy, fragrant, dewy!
See the rainbow shower!
Was there e'er so sweet a flower?
I'm the rose-nymph, June they call me.
Sunset's blush is not more fair
Than the gift of bloom so rare,
Mortal, that I bring to thee!

July

Sunshine and shadow play amid the trees
In bosky groves, while from the vivid sky
The sun's gold arrows fleck the fields at noon,
Where weary cattle to their slumber hie.
How sweet the music of the purling rill,
Trickling adown the grassy hill!
While dreamy fancies come to give repose
When the first star of evening glows.

August

Haste to the mighty ocean,
List to the lapsing waves;
With what a strange commotion
They seek their coral caves.
From heat and turmoil let us oft return,
The ocean's solemn majesty to learn.

September

With what a gentle sound
The autumn leaves drop to the ground;
The many-colored dyes,
They greet our watching eyes.
Rosy and russet, how they fall!
Throwing o'er earth a leafy pall.

October

The mellow moon hangs golden in the sky,
The vintage song is over, far and nigh
A richer beauty Nature weareth now,
And silently, in reverence we bow
Before the forest altars, off'ring praise
To Him who sweetness gives to all our days.

November

The leaves are sere,
The woods are drear,
The breeze that erst so merrily did play,
Naught giveth save a melancholy lay;
Yet life's great lessons do not fail
E'en in November's gale.

December

List! list! the sleigh bells peal across the snow;
The frost's sharp arrows touch the earth and lo!
How diamond-bright the stars do scintillate
When Night hath lit her lamps to Heaven's gate.
To the dim forest's cloistered arches go,
And seek the holly and the mistletoe;
For soon the bells of Christmas-tide will ring
To hail the Heavenly King!

THE COLORED CADET AT WEST POINT

LIEUT. HENRY OSSIAN FLIPPER, U. S. A.

May 20th, 1873! Auspicious day! From the deck of the little ferry-boat that steamed its way across from Garrison's on that eventful afternoon I viewed the hills about West Point, her stone structures perched thereon, thus rising still higher, as if providing access to the very pinnacle of fame, and shuddered. With my mind full of the horrors of the treatment of all former cadets of color, and the dread of inevitable ostracism, I approached tremblingly yet confidently.

The little vessel having been moored, I stepped ashore and inquired of a soldier there where candidates should report. He very kindly gave me all information, wished me much success, for which I thanked him, and set out for the designated place. I soon reached it, and walked directly into the adjutant's office. He received me kindly, asked for my certificate of appointment, and receiving that—or assurance that I had it—I do not remember which—directed me to write in a book there for the purpose the name and occupation of my father, the State, Congressional district, county and city of his residence, my own full name, age, State, county, and place of my birth, and my occupation when at home. This done I was sent in charge of an orderly to cadet barracks, where my "plebe quarters" were assigned me.

The impression made upon me by what I saw while going from the adjutant's office to barracks was certainly not very encouraging. The rear windows were crowded with cadets watching my unpretending passage of the area of barracks with apparently as much astonishment and interest as they would, perhaps, have watched Hannibal crossing the Alps. Their words and jeers were most insulting.

Having reached another office, I was shown in by the orderly. I walked in, hat in hand—nay, rather started in—when three cadets, who were seated in the room, simultaneously sprang to their feet and welcomed me somewhat after this fashion:

"Well, sir, what do you mean by coming into this office in that manner, sir? Get out of here, sir."

I walked out, followed by one of them, who, in a similar strain, ordered me to button my coat, get my hands around—"fins" he said—heels together, and head up.

"Now, sir," said he, leaving me, "when you are ready to come in, knock at that door," emphasizing the word "knock."

The door was open. I knocked. He replied, "Come in." I went in. I took my position in front of and facing him, my heels together, head up, the palms of my hands to the front, and my little fingers on the seams of my pantaloons, in which position we habitually carried them. After correcting my position and making it sufficiently military to suit himself, one of them, in a much milder tone, asked what I desired of them. I told him I had been sent by the adjutant to report there. He arose, and directing me to follow him, conducted me to the bath-rooms. Having discharged the necessary duty there, I returned and was again put in charge of the orderly, who carried me to the hospital. There I was subjected to a rigid physical examination, which I "stood" with the greatest ease. I was given a certificate of ability by the surgeon, and by him sent again to the adjutant, who in turn sent me to the treasurer. From him I returned alone to barracks.

The reception given to "plebes" upon reporting is often very much more severe than that given me. Even members of my own class can testify to this. This reception has, however, I think, been best described in an anonymous work, where it is thus set forth:

"How dare you come into the presence of your superior officer in that grossly careless and unmilitary manner? I'll have you imprisoned. Stand, attention, sir!" (Even louder than before.) "Heels-together-and-on-the-same-line, toes-equally-turned-out, little-fingers-on-the-seams-of-your-pantaloons, button-your-coat, draw-in-your-chin, throw-out-your-chest, cast-your-eyes-fifteen-paces-to-the-front, don't-let-me-see-you-wearing-standing-collars-again. Stand-steady, sir. You've evidently mistaken your profession, sir. In any other service, or at the seat of war, sir, you would have been shot, sir, without trial, sir, for such conduct, sir."

The effect of such words can be easily imagined. A "plebe" will at once recognize the necessity for absolute obedience, even if he does know all this is hazing, and that it is doubtless forbidden. Still "plebes" almost invariably tremble while it lasts, and when in their own quarters laugh over it, and even practise it upon each other for mutual amusement.

On the way to barracks I met the squad of "beasts" marching to dinner. I was ordered to fall in, did so, marched to the mess hall, and ate my first dinner at West Point. After dinner we were again marched to barracks and dismissed. I hastened to my quarters, and a short while after was turned out to take possession of my baggage. I lugged it into my room, was shown the directions on the back of the door for arrangement of articles, and ordered to obey them within half an hour.

At the end of the time specified every article was arranged and the cadet corporal returned to inspect. He walked deliberately to the clothes-press, and, informing me that everything was arranged wrong, threw every article upon the floor, repeated his order and withdrew. And thus three times in less than two hours did I arrange and he disarrange my effects. I was not troubled again by him till after supper, when he inspected again, merely opening the door, however, and looking in. He told me I could not go to sleep till "tattoo." Now tattoo, as he evidently used it, referred in some manner to time, and with such reference I had not the remotest idea of what it meant. I had no knowledge whatever of military terms or customs. However, as I was also told that I could do anything—writing, etc.—I might wish to do, I found sufficient to keep me awake until he again returned and told me it was then tattoo, that I could retire then or at any time within half an hour, and that at the end of that time the light *must* be extinguished and I *must* be in bed. I instantly extinguished it and retired.

Thus passed my first half day at West Point, and thus began the military career of the fifth colored cadet. The other four were Smith of South Carolina, Napier of Tennessee, Howard of Mississippi, and Gibbs of Florida.

AN HYMN TO THE EVENING

PHYLLIS WHEATLEY

Soon as the sun forsook the eastern main
The pealing thunder shook the heav'nly plain;
Majestic grandeur! From the zephyr's wing,
Exhales the incense of the blooming spring.
Soft purl the streams, the birds renew their notes,
And through the air their mingled music floats,
Through all the heav'ns what beauteous dyes are spread!
But the west glories in the deepest red;
So may our breasts with every virtue glow
The living temples of our God below!
Filled with the praise of him who gave the light,
And draws the sable curtains of the night,
Let placid slumbers soothe each weary mind,
At morn to wake more heaven'ly, more refin'd.
So shall the labors of the day begin
More pure, more guarded from the snares of sin.
Nights' leaden sceptor seal my drowsy eyes,
When cease my song, till fair Aurora rise.

GOING TO SCHOOL UNDER DIFFICULTIES

WILLIAM H. HOLTZCLAW

When I was four years old I was put to work on the farm,—that is, at such work as I could do, such as riding a deaf and blind mule while my brother held the plow. When I was six years old my four-year-old brother and I had to go two miles through a lonely forest every morning in order to carry my father's breakfast and dinner to a sawmill, where he was hauling logs for sixty cents a day. The white man, Frank Weathers, who employed a large number of hands, both Negroes and whites, was considered one of the best and most upright men in that section of the country.

In those days there were no public schools in that part of the country for the Negroes. Indeed, public schools for whites were just beginning to be established. This man set aside a little house in the neighborhood of the sawmill, employed a teacher, and urged all the Negroes to send their children to this school. Not a great many of them, however, took advantage of his generosity, for this was at the time when everybody seemed to think that the Negro's only hope was in politics.

But my father and mother had great faith in education, and they were determined that their children should have that blessing of which they themselves had been deprived.

Soon, however, Mr. Weathers had cut all the timber that he could get in that section, and he therefore moved his mills to another district. This left us without a school. But my father was not to be outdone. He called a meeting of the men in that community, and they agreed to build a schoolhouse themselves. They went to the forest and cut pine poles about eight inches in diameter, split them in halves, and carried them on their shoulders to a nice shady spot, and there erected a little schoolhouse. The benches were made of the same material, and there was no floor nor chimney. Some of the other boys' trousers suffered when they sat on the new pine benches, which exuded rosin, but I had an advantage of them in this respect, for I wore only a shirt. In fact, I never wore trousers until I got to be so large that the white neighbors complained of my insufficient clothes.

At the end of the first school year there was a trying time in our family. On this occasion the teacher ordered all the pupils to appear dressed in white. We had no white clothes, nor many of any other sort, for that matter. Father and mother discussed our predicament nearly all one night. Father said it was foolish to buy clothes which could be used for that occasion only. But my ever resourceful mother was still determined that her children should look as well on this important occasion as any of our neighbors. However, when we went to bed the night before the exhibition we still had no white clothes and no cloth from which to make them. Nevertheless, when we awoke the next morning, all three of us had beautiful white suits.

It came about in this way. My mother had a beautiful white Sunday petticoat, which she had cut up and made into suits for us. As there is just so much cloth in a petticoat and no more, the stuff had to be cut close to cover all of us children, and as the petticoat had been worn several times and was, therefore, likely to tear, we had to be very careful how we stooped in moving about the stage, lest there should be a general splitting and tearing, with consequences that we were afraid to imagine. At the exhibitions the next night we said our little pieces, and I suppose we looked about as well as the others; at least we thought so, and that was sufficient. One thing I am sure of,—there was no mother there who was prouder of her children than ours. The thing that made her so pleased was the fact that my speech made such an impression that our white landlord lifted me off the stage when I had finished speaking and gave me a quarter of a dollar.

If there happened to be a school in the winter time, I had sometimes to go bare-footed and always with scant clothing. Our landlady was very kind in such cases. She would give me clothes that had already been worn by her sons, and in turn I would bring broom straw from the sedges, with which she made her brooms. In this way I usually got enough clothes to keep me warm.

So, with my mother's encouragement, I went to school in spite of my bare feet. Often the ground would be frozen, and often there would be snow. My feet would crack and bleed freely, but when I reached home Mother would have a tub full of hot water ready to plunge me into and thaw me out. Although this caused my feet and legs to swell, it usually got me into shape for school the next day.

I remember once, when I had helped "lay by" the crops at home and was ready to enter the little one-month school, it was decided that I could not go, because I had no hat. My mother told me that if I could catch a 'coon and cure the skin, she would make me a cap out of that material. That night I went far into the forest with my hounds, and finally located a 'coon. The 'coon was a mighty fighter, and when he had driven off all my dogs I saw that the only chance for me to get a cap was to whip the 'coon myself, so together with the dogs I went at him, and finally we conquered him. The next week I went to school wearing my new 'coon-skin cap.

Exertions of this kind, from time to time, strengthened my will and my body, and prepared me for more trying tests which were to come later.

As I grew older it became more and more difficult for me to go to school. When cotton first began to open,—early in the fall,—it brought a higher price than at any other time of the year. At this time the landlord wanted us all to stop school and pick cotton. But Mother wanted me to remain in school, so, when the landlord came to the quarters early in the morning to stir up the cotton pickers, she used to outgeneral him by hiding me behind the skillets, ovens, and pots, throwing some old rags over me until he was gone. Then she would slip me off to school through the back way. I can see her now with her hands upon my shoulder, shoving me along through the woods and underbrush, in a roundabout way, keeping me all the time out of sight of the great plantation until we reached the point, a mile away from home, where we came to the public road. There my mother would bid me good-bye, whereupon she would return to the plantation and try to make up to the landlord for the work of us both in the field as cotton pickers.

THE BRAVE SON

ALSTON W. BURLEIGH

A little boy, lost in his childish play,
Mid the deep'ning shades of the fading day,
Fancied the warrior he would be;
He scattered his foes with his wooden sword
And put to flight a mighty horde—
Ere he crept to his daddy's knee.

A soldier crawled o'er the death-strewn plain,
And he uttered the name of his love, in vain,
As he stumbled over the crest;
He fought with the fierceness of dark despair
And drove the cowering foe to his lair—
Ere he crept to his Father's breast.

VICTORY

WALTER F. WHITE

"Now, Ted, just forget they're after you and remember you've got ten men out there with you. Fight 'em and fight 'em hard, but hold that man-eating temper of yours. If you don't, we're lost."

Dawson, varsity coach of Bliss University, affectionately known and revered by two thousand undergraduates as "Skipper Bill" sat in the locker room with his arm around Ted Robertson's shoulders, star halfback and punter of the varsity eleven. Around them moved the other varsity players, substitutes, second string men, trainers and rubbers.

In the stands overhead every seat was taken, for these were the last few minutes before the big game of the year—the annual battle with Sloan College. On one side the sober blues and grays and blacks formed a background for huge yellow chrysanthemums and light blue ribbons, the Bliss colors, and the same background in the stands opposite set off the crimson of Sloan College.

The rival college bands of the two most important colored universities of the United States blared almost unheeded in the din, while agile cheerleaders clad in white from head to foot performed gymnastics in leading rolling volumes of cheers. All were in that tense, nerve-gripping mood prior to that game in which victory or defeat meant success or failure of the season's efforts of the teams of young giants that represented the two schools.

In the locker room, however, a different scene was being enacted. Every man was acting according to his own temperament and each in his own way attempted to hide the anxious thrill that every real football player feels before "the big game."

Jimmy Murray, quarterback and thrower of forward passes *par excellence*, nervously tied and untied his shoe laces a dozen times; "Tiny" Marshall, left tackle, who weighed two hundred and ten pounds, tried to whistle nonchalantly and failed miserably, while "Bull" Bascom, fullback, the only calm man in the room, was carefully adjusting his shoulder pads. Around them hovered the odor of arnica and liniment mixed with the familiar tang of perspiration which has dried in woolen jerseys—perspiration that marked many a long and wearisome hour of training and perfection of the machine that to-day received its final "exam."

Ted Robertson, the man around whom most of the team's offense was built, sat listening to Dawson's advice. Born with a fiery, almost unmanageable temper, his reckless, dauntless spirit had made him a terror to opposing teams. Strong was the line that could check his plunges, and fleet were the ends who could tackle him when once he got loose in an open field. Recognizing his phenomenal ability, both coach and players gave him the credit due him and consciously or unconsciously relied on him as the team's best player.

But to-day Sloan had declared that they were going to put Robertson out of the game and threats had been freely uttered that before the game had been going very long he "would be in the hospital." This news added to the tenseness of feeling. If Robertson should be put out of the game, or if he should lose his temper the chances of a victory for Bliss were slim indeed, for rarely had two teams been so evenly matched in skill and brain and brawn. Thus the final pleading of Dawson to Robertson to "hold that temper."

A roar of cheers greeted their ears as the red jerseyed Sloan team took the field. Led by Murray the Bliss players were likewise greeted by a storm of applause as they trotted out on the field and the varsity started through a brisk signal drill.

In a few minutes the referee called the rival captains to the center of the field. Sloan won the toss and elected to defend the south goal, kicking off with the wind behind its back. A breathless hush—the shrill whistle of the referee—the thump of cleated shoe against the ball and the game was on.

The teams, wonderfully even in strength and in knowledge of the game, surged back and forth, the ball repeatedly changing hands as one team would hold the other for downs. From the kick-off, the Sloan players began their attempts to injure or anger Robertson. Vicious remarks were aimed at him while the referee was not near enough to hear.

When Robertson carried the ball and after he was downed under a mass of players, a fist would thud against his jaw or hard knuckles would be rubbed across his nose. Once when an opposing player had fallen across Robertson's right leg, another of his opponents seized his ankle and turned it. Though he fought against it, his temper was slowly but surely slipping away from him.

For three hectic quarters, with the tide of victory or defeat now surging towards Bliss—now towards Sloan, the battle raged. As play after play of brilliance or superbrilliance flashed forth, the stands alternately groaned or cheered, according to the sympathies of each. Robertson, a veritable stonewall of defense, time and again checked the rushes of the Sloan backs or threw himself recklessly at fleet backs on end runs when his own ends had failed to "get their man." On the offensive he repeatedly was called on to carry the ball and seldom did he fail to make the distance required.

A great weariness settled on Robertson and it was with difficulty that he was able to fight off a numbness and dizziness that almost overcame him. One thing sustained him. It was a bitter resentment against those who sought to hurt him. The fires within him had grown until they became a flaming, devastating thing that burned its way into his brain. It needed only a spark to make him forget the game, school, the coach and everything else. Yet even as he realized this he knew that if he did lose his temper, Bliss might as well concede the victory to Sloan. It was not conceit that caused him to know this and admit it but the clearness of vision that comes oft-times in a moment of greatest mental strain.

Finally, with the score still tied, neither side having scored, the time keeper warned the rival teams that only three minutes remained for play. His warning served to cause a tightening of muscles and a grimness of countenance in a last final effort to put over a score and avert a tied score. The huge crowd prayed fervently for a score—a touchdown—a safety—a goal from field or placement—anything.

It was Sloan's ball on Bliss's forty-five-yard line. Only a fumble or some fluke could cause a score. Every player was on his mettle burning with anxiety to get his hands on that ball and scamper down the field to a touchdown and everlasting fame in the annals of his school's football history.

In a last desperate effort, the Bliss quarterback called a trick play. It started out like a quarterback run around left end. The Bliss left end ran straight down the field after delaying the man playing opposite him. When the Bliss quarter had made a wide run drawing in the Sloan secondary defense, he turned and like a flash shot a long forward pass over the heads of the incoming Sloan backfield to the end who had gone straight down the field and who was practically free of danger of being tackled by any of the Sloan backs.

Too late the Sloan players saw the ruse. Only Robertson was between the swift running end and a score. With grim satisfaction, his face streaked with perspiration, drawn and weary with the long hard struggle and the yeoman part he had played in it, Robertson saw that the man with the ball was the one player on the opposing side who had done most of the unfair playing in trying to put Robertson out of the game. All of the bitterness—all of the anger in his heart swelled up and he determined to overtake the end, prevent the score and tackle the man so viciously that he would be certain to break an arm or a leg. Robertson dug his cleats in the spongy turf with a phenomenal burst of speed, rapidly overtook his man, driving him meanwhile towards the sidelines.

At last the moment came. By making a flying tackle, which would be illegal but which he hoped the referee would not see, Robertson could get his man and get him in such fashion that he would have no chance of escaping injury. Robertson crouched for the spring. A fierce light came into his eyes. In a flash he saw the end whom he now hated with an intensity that wiped every thought from his mind except that of revenge, lying prone on the ground.

But even as he gloated over his revenge, the words of Bill Dawson came to him, "Hold that man-eating temper of yours." In a lightning-like conflict, the impulse to injure fought a desperate battle with the instinct of clean playing. His decision was made in a moment. Instead of making the vicious flying tackle, he ran all the faster, but the end was too swift and had too great a lead. Amid the frantically jubilant shouts of the Bliss rooters and the painful silence of the Sloan supporters the end went across the line for a touchdown just as time was up.

A gloom pervaded the dressing rooms of the Sloan team after the game. Robertson was in disgrace. Forgotten was the playing through most of the game. Forgotten were his desperate tackles that had saved the game more than once. Forgotten were the long runs and the hard line plunges that time and again had made first downs for his team. Only the fact that he had apparently failed in the last minute remained. Only Dawson and Robertson knew that it was not cowardice, that most detested of all things in athletics, in life itself, had caused Robertson to refuse to make that last dangerous, illegal flying tackle.

But in the heart of Robertson there was a strange peace. Being human, he naturally resented the discernible thoughts in the minds of his comrades of many a hard-fought battle. But a calmness made him forgetful of all this for he knew that at last, in a moment of the supreme test, he had conquered that which had been his master throughout all of his life—his temper. All the slurs and coldness in the world could not rob him of the satisfaction of this.

THE DOG AND THE CLEVER RABBIT

A. O. STAFFORD

There were many days when the animals did not think about the kingship. They thought of their games and their tricks, and would play them from the rising to the setting of the sun.

Now, at that time, the little rabbit was known as a very clever fellow. His tricks, his schemes, and his funny little ways caused much mischief and at times much anger among his woodland cousins.

At last the wolf made up his mind to catch him and give him a severe punishment for the many tricks he had played upon him.

Knowing that the rabbit could run faster than he, the wolf called at the home of the dog to seek his aid. "Brother dog, frisky little rabbit must be caught and punished. For a nice bone will you help me?" asked the wolf.

"Certainly, my good friend," answered the dog, thinking of the promised bone.

"Be very careful, the rabbit is very clever," said the wolf as he left.

A day or so later while passing through the woods the dog saw the rabbit frisking in the tall grass. Quick as a flash the dog started after him. The little fellow ran and, to save himself, jumped into the hollow of an oak tree. The opening was too small for the other to follow and as he looked in he heard only the merry laugh of the frisky rabbit, "Hee, hee! hello, Mr. Dog, you can't see me."

"Never mind, boy, I will get you yet," barked the angry dog.

A short distance from the tree a goose was seen moving around looking for her dinner.

"Come, friend goose, watch the hollow of this tree while I go and get some moss and fire to smoke out this scamp of a rabbit," spoke the dog, remembering the advice of the wolf.

"Of course I'll watch, for he has played many of his schemes upon me," returned the bird.

When the dog left, the rabbit called out from his hiding place, "How can you watch, friend goose, when you can't see me?"

"Well, I will see you then," she replied. With these words she pushed her long neck into the hollow of the tree. As the neck of the goose went into the opening the rabbit threw the dust of some dry wood into her eyes.

"Oh, oh, you little scamp, you have made me blind," cried out the bird in pain.

Then while the goose was trying to get the dust from her eyes the rabbit jumped out and scampered away.

In a short while the dog returned with the moss and fire, filled the opening, and, as he watched the smoke arise, barked with glee, "Now I have you, my tricky friend, now I have you." But as no rabbit ran out the dog turned to the goose and saw from her red, streaming eyes that something was wrong.

"Where is the rabbit, friend goose?" he quickly asked.

"Why, he threw wood dust into my eyes when I peeped into the opening." At once the dog knew that the rabbit had escaped and became very angry.

"You silly goose, you foolish bird with web feet, I will kill you now for such folly." With these words the dog sprang for the goose, but only a small feather was caught in his mouth as the frightened bird rose high in the air and flew away.

THE BOY AND THE IDEAL

JOSEPH S. COTTER

Once upon a time a Mule, a Hog, a Snake, and a Boy met. Said the Mule: "I eat and labor that I may grow strong in the heels. It is fine to have heels so gifted. My heels make people cultivate distance."

Said the Hog: "I eat and labor that I may grow strong in the snout. It is fine to have a fine snout. I keep people watching for my snout."

"No exchanging heels for snouts," broke in the Mule.

"No," answered the Hog; "snouts are naturally above heels."

Said the Snake: "I eat to live, and live to cultivate my sting. The way people shun me shows my greatness. Beget stings, comrades, and stings will beget glory."

Said the Boy: "There is a star in my life like unto a star in the sky. I eat and labor that I may think aright and feel aright. These rounds will conduct me to my star. Oh, inviting star!"

"I am not so certain of that," said the Mule. "I have noticed your kind and ever see some of myself in them. Your star is in the distance."

The Boy answered by smelling a flower and listening to the song of a bird. The Mule looked at him and said: "He is all tenderness and care. The true and the beautiful have robbed me of a kinsman. His star is near."

Said the Boy: "I approach my star."

"I am not so certain of that," interrupted the Hog. "I have noticed your kind and I ever see some of myself in them. Your star is a delusion."

The Boy answered by painting the flower and setting the notes of the bird's song to music.

The Hog looked at the boy and said: "His soul is attuned by nature. The meddler in him is slain."

"I can all but touch my star," cried the Boy.

"I am not so certain of that," remarked the Snake. "I have watched your kind and ever see some of myself in them. Stings are nearer than stars."

The Boy answered by meditating upon the picture and music. The Snake departed, saying that stings and stars cannot keep company.

The Boy journeyed on, ever led by the star. Some distance away the Mule was bemoaning the presence of his heels and trying to rid himself of them by kicking a tree. The Hog was dividing his time between looking into a brook and rubbing his snout on a rock to shorten it. The Snake lay dead of its own bite. The Boy journeyed on, led by an ever inviting star.

CHILDREN AT EASTER

C. EMILY FRAZIER

That day in old Jerusalem when Christ our Lord was slain,
I wonder if the children hid and wept in grief and pain;
Dear little ones, on whose fair brows His tender touch had been,
Whose infant forms had nestled close His loving arms within.

I think that very soberly went mournful little feet
When Christ our Lord was laid away in Joseph's garden sweet,

Children At Easter

And wistful eyes grew very sad and dimpled cheeks grew white,
When He who suffered babes to come was prisoned from the light.

With beaming looks and eager words a glad surprise He gave
To those who sought their buried Lord and found an empty grave;
For truly Christ had conquered death, Himself the Prince of Life,
And none of all His Followers shall fail in any strife.

O little ones, around the cross your Easter garlands twine,
And bring your precious Easter gifts to many a sacred shrine,
And, better still, let offerings of pure young hearts be given
On Easter Day to Him who reigns the King of earth and heaven.

ABRAHAM LINCOLN

WILLIAM PICKENS

He was the first President of the Republic who was American through and through. There was not one foreign element in his bringing up; he was an unmixed child of the Western plains, born in the South, reared in the North. Most of the Presidents before him, being reared nearer the Atlantic, had imbibed more or less of Eastern culture and had European airs. This man Lincoln was so thoroughly democratic as to astonish both Old and New England. He never acted "the President," and was always a man among men, the honored servant of the people.

From a five-dollar fee before a justice of the peace, he had risen to a five-thousand-dollar fee before the Supreme Court of Illinois. From a study of "Dilworth's Spelling Book" in his seventh year, he had risen to write, in his fifty-seventh year, his second Inaugural, which is the greatest utterance of man, and yet all of his days in school added together are less than one year. His pioneer life had given him a vein of humor which became his "Life-preserver" in times of stress; it had also given him a love for human liberty that was unaffected. He felt that the enslavement of some men was but the advance guard, the miner and sapper, of the enslavement of all men.

From a poor captain of volunteers in the scandalous little Black Hawk War, where he jokingly said he "bled, died, and came away," although he never had a skirmish nor saw an Indian, he had risen to the chief command in a war that numbered three thousand battles and skirmishes and cost three billion dollars. Having no ancestry himself, being able to trace his line by rumor and tradition only as far back as his grandfather, he became, like George Washington, the Father of his Country. Born of a father who could not write his name, he himself had written the Proclamation of Emancipation, the fourth great state paper in the history of the Anglo-Saxon race,—the others being Magna Charta, the Declaration of Independence and the Constitution. If we accept the statement of Cicero that the days on which we are saved should be as illustrious as the days on which we are born, then Lincoln the Savior must always remain coördinate with Washington, the Father of his country. Jackson was "Old Hickory," Taylor was "Old Rough," and there have been various names given to the other Presidents, but Washington and Lincoln were the only ones whom the American people styled "Father."

Child of the American soil, cradled and nursed in the very bosom of nature, he loved his country with the passion with which most men love their human mothers. He could not bear the thought of one iota of detraction from her honor, her dignity or her welfare. Against her dismemberment he was willing to fight to the end of his second administration or till the end of time. He might tolerate anything else except disunion,—even the right of some of his fellowmen to enslave others. Of every concession which he made during his administration, to friend or foe, the *sine qua non* was Union. A house divided against itself cannot stand.

In this he left us a great heritage; it is a lesson for both sections, and all races of any section. White men of America, black men of America, by the eternal God of heaven, there can be no division of destiny on the same soil and in the bosom and in the lap of the same natural mother. Men may attempt and accomplish discrimination in a small way, but Almighty God and all-mothering nature are absolutely impartial. They have woven the fabric of life so that the thread of each man's existence is a part of the whole. He who sets fire to his neighbor's house, endangers the existence of his own; he who degrades his neighbor's children, undermines the future of his own. Together we rise and together we fall is the plan of God and the rule of nature. We must lean together in the common struggle of life: the syncline is stronger than the anticline.

In a great nation with an increasing fame, the lesson of Lincoln's life must grow in importance. As long as the human heart loves freedom his name will be a word on the tongues of men. His name will be a watchword wherever liberty in her struggles with tyranny lifts her embattled banners. No man of the ancient or the modern world has a securer place in the hearts and memories of men than this man Lincoln, who was born in obscurity, who died in a halo, and who now rests in an aureole of historic glory.

RONDEAU

JESSIE FAUSET

When April's here and meadows wide
Once more with spring's sweet growths are pied,
I close each book, drop each pursuit,
And past the brook, no longer mute,
I joyous roam the countryside.

Look, here the violets shy abide
And there the mating robins hide—
How keen my senses, how acute,
When April's here!

And list! down where the shimmering tide
Hard by that farthest hill doth glide,
Rise faint sweet strains from shepherd's flute,
Pan's pipes and Berecynthian lute.
Each sight, each sound fresh joys provide
When April's here.

HOW I ESCAPED

FREDERICK DOUGLASS

Although slavery was a delicate subject, and very cautiously talked about among grown-up people in Maryland, I frequently talked about it, and that very freely, with the white boys. I would sometimes say to them, while seated on a curbstone or a cellar door, "I wish I could be free, as you will be when you get to be men. You will be free, you know, as soon as you are twenty-one, and can go where you like, but I am a slave for life. Have I not as good a right to be free as you have?"

Words like these, I observed, always troubled them; and I had no small satisfaction in drawing out from them, as I occasionally did, that fresh and bitter condemnation of slavery which ever springs from natures unseared and unperverted. Of all consciences, let me have those to deal with, which have not been seared and bewildered with the cares and perplexities of life.

I do not remember ever to have met with a boy while I was in slavery, who defended the system, but I do remember many times, when I was consoled by them, and by them encouraged to hope that something would yet occur by which I would be made free. Over and over again, they have told me that "they believed I had as good a right to be free as they had," and that "they did not believe God ever made any one to be a slave."

On Monday, the third day of September, 1838, in accordance with my resolution, I bade farewell to the city of Baltimore, and to slavery.

My success was due to address rather than courage; to good luck rather than bravery. My means of escape were provided for me by the very men who were making laws to hold and bind me more securely in slavery. It was the custom in the State of Maryland to require of the free colored people to have what were called free papers. This instrument they were required to renew very often, and by charging a fee for this writing, considerable sums from time to time were collected by the State. In these papers the name, age, color, height, and form of the free man were described, together with any scars or other marks upon his person.

Now more than one man could be found to answer the same general description. Hence many slaves could escape by impersonating the owner of one set of papers; and this was often done as follows: A slave nearly or sufficiently answering the description set forth in the papers, would borrow or hire them till he could by their means escape to a free state, and then, by mail or otherwise, return them to the owner. The operation was a hazardous one for the lender as well as the borrower.

A failure on the part of the fugitive to send back the papers would imperil his benefactor, and the discovery of the papers in possession of the wrong man would imperil both the fugitive and his friend. It was therefore an act of supreme trust on the part of a freeman of color thus to put in jeopardy his own liberty that another might be free. It was, however, not infrequently bravely done, and was seldom discovered. I was not so fortunate as to sufficiently resemble any of my free acquaintances to answer the description of their papers.

But I had one friend—a sailor—who owned a sailor's protection, which answered somewhat the purpose of free papers—describing his person, and certifying to the fact that he was a free American sailor. The instrument had at its head the American eagle, which gave it the appearance at once of an authorized document. This protection did not, when in my hands, describe its bearer very accurately. Indeed, it called for a man much darker than myself, and close examination of it would have caused my arrest at the start.

In order to avoid this fatal scrutiny I had arranged with a hackman to bring my baggage to the train just on the moment of starting, and jumped upon the car myself when the train was already in motion. Had I gone into the station and offered to purchase a ticket, I should have been instantly and carefully examined, and undoubtedly arrested.

In choosing this plan upon which to act, I considered the jostle of the train, and the natural haste of the conductor, in a train crowded with passengers, and relied upon my skill and address in playing the sailor as described in my protection, to do the rest. One element in my favor was the kind feeling which prevailed in Baltimore, and other seaports at the time, towards "those who go down to the sea in ships." "Free trade and sailors' rights" expressed the sentiment of the country just then.

In my clothing I was rigged out in sailor style. I had on a red shirt and a tarpaulin hat and black cravat, tied in sailor fashion, carelessly and loosely about my neck. My knowledge of ships and sailor's talk came much to my assistance, for I knew a ship from stem to stern, and from keelson to cross-trees, and could talk sailor like an "old salt."

On sped the train, and I was well on the way to Havre de Grace before the conductor came into the Negro car to collect tickets and examine the papers of his black passengers. This was a critical moment in the drama. My whole future depended upon the decision of this conductor. Agitated I was while this ceremony was proceeding, but still externally, at least, I was apparently calm and self-possessed. He went on with his duty—examining several colored passengers before reaching me. He was somewhat harsh in tone, and peremptory in manner until he reached me, when, strangely enough, and to my surprise and relief, his whole manner changed.

Seeing that I did not readily produce my free papers, as the other colored persons in the car had done, he said to me in a friendly contrast with that observed towards the others: "I suppose you have your free papers?" To which I answered: "No, sir; I never carry my free papers to sea with me." "But you have something to show that you are a free man, have you not?" "Yes, sir," I answered; "I have a paper with the American eagle on it, that will carry me around the world." With this I drew from my deep sailor's pocket my seaman's protection, as before described. The merest glance at the paper satisfied him, and he took my fare and went on about his business.

This moment of time was one of the most anxious I ever experienced. Had the conductor looked closely at the paper, he could not have failed to discover that it called for a very different looking person from myself, and in that case it would have been his duty to arrest me on the instant, and send me back to Baltimore from the first station.

When he left me with the assurance that I was all right, though much relieved, I realized that I was still in great danger: I was still in Maryland, and subject to arrest at any moment. I saw on the train several persons who would have known me in any other clothes, and I feared they might recognize me, even in my sailor "rig," and report me to the conductor, who would then subject me to a closer examination, which I knew well would be fatal to me.

Though I was not a murderer fleeing from justice, I felt, perhaps, quite miserable as such a criminal. The train was moving at a very high rate of speed for that time of railroad travel, but to my anxious mind, it was moving far too slowly. Minutes were hours, and hours were days during this part of my flight. After Maryland I was to pass through Delaware—another slave State. The border lines between slavery and freedom were the dangerous ones, for the fugitives. The heart of no fox or deer, with hungry hounds on his trail, in full chase, could have beaten more anxiously or noisily than did mine, from the time I left Baltimore till I reached Philadelphia.

The passage of the Susquehanna river at Havre de Grace was made by ferry-boat at that time, on board of which I met a young colored man by the name of Nichols, who came very near betraying me. He was a "hand" on the boat, but instead of minding his business, he insisted upon knowing me, and asking me dangerous questions as to where I was going, and when I was coming back, etc. I got away from my old and inconvenient acquaintance as soon as I could decently do so, and went to another part of the boat.

Once across the river I encountered a new danger. Only a few days before I had been at work on a revenue cutter, in Mr. Price's ship-yard, under the care of Captain McGowan. On the meeting at this point of the two trains, the one going south stopped on the track just opposite to the one going north, and it so happened that this Captain McGowan sat at a window where he could see me very distinctly, and would certainly have recognized me had he looked at me but for a second. Fortunately, in the hurry of the moment, he did not see me; and the trains soon passed each other on their respective ways.

But this was not the only hair-breadth escape. A German blacksmith, whom I knew well, was on the train with me, and looked at me very intently, as if he thought he had seen me somewhere before in his travels. I really believe he knew me, but had no heart to betray me. At any rate he saw me escaping and held his peace.

The last point of imminent danger, and the one I dreaded most, was Wilmington. Here we left the train and took the steamboat for Philadelphia. In making the change here I again apprehended arrest, but no one disturbed me, and I was soon on the broad and beautiful Delaware, speeding away to the Quaker City. On reaching Philadelphia in the afternoon I inquired of a colored man how I could get on to New York? He directed me to the Willow street depot, and thither I went, taking the train that night. I reached New York Tuesday morning, having completed the journey in less than twenty-four hours. Such is briefly the manner of my escape from slavery—and the end of my experience as a slave.

FREDERICK DOUGLASS

W. H. CROGMAN

Frederick Douglass is dead! How strange that sounds to those of us who from earliest boyhood have been accustomed to hear him spoken of as the living exponent of all that is noblest and best in the race. The mind reluctantly accepts the unwelcome truth. And yet it is a truth—a serious, a solemn truth. Frederick Douglass is no more. The grand old hero of a thousand battles has at last fallen before the shaft of the common destroyer, and upon his well-battered shield loving hands have tenderly borne that stalwart form to its last, long resting place. Earth to earth, dust to dust, ashes to ashes!

This country will never again see another Douglass; this world will never again see another Douglass, for in all probability there will never again exist that peculiar combination of circumstances to produce exactly such a type of manhood. Man is, in a measure, the product of environment. Yet it would be injustice to Frederick Douglass to say that he was great simply because of environment. He was great in spite of environment. Born a slave, subjected in his youth and early manhood to all the degrading, stultifying, demoralizing influences of slavery, he has left behind him, after a public life long and varied and stormy, a name as clean and spotless as driven snow. Take notice of this, young men, you who have ambitions, you who are aspiring to public place, position, and power. Take notice that a public life need not be separated from unsullied honor.

I said Frederick Douglass was great in spite of environment. Had there been no slavery to fight, no freedom to win, he would still have been a great man. Greatness was inherent in his being, and circumstances simply evoked it. He was one of those choice spirits whom the Almighty sends into this world with the stamp of a great mission on their very form and features. Said Sam Johnson with reference to Edmund Burke: "Burke, sir, is such a man that if you met him for the first time in the street, where you were stopped by a drove of oxen, and you and he stepped aside to take shelter but for five minutes, he'd talk to you in such a manner that when you parted you would say, 'This is an extraordinary man.'"

The same could doubtless have been said of Douglass; but it was not necessary to hear him talk, to discover his unusual ability and surpassing intelligence. There was in his very presence something that instantly indicated these. An eminent divine said some years ago that Douglass's escape from slavery was a very fortunate thing for the South, as in any uprising of slaves he must have proved a very formidable leader. "He had," said he, "the mind to plan, the heart to dare, and the hand to execute," and added, "If you were to see him sitting in Exeter Hall in the midst of a sea of faces, you would instantly recognize in him a man of extraordinary force of character."

Such was the impression that Douglass commonly made on people, and such was the impression he made on me at my first sight of him. It was in Faneuil Hall, in the summer of 1872. The colored people of New England were assembled in political convention. Entering the hall in the midst of one of their morning sessions, the first object that met my eyes was the old hero himself on the rostrum. There he stood, over six feet in height, erect, broad-shouldered, deep-chested, with massive, well-formed head, covered with thick, bushy hair, about half gray. I judged him then to be midway in his fifties. His face, strongly leonine, was clean shaven, except moustache, while those eyes, that even in the seventies could flash fire, lighted up the whole countenance, and made the general effect such as not to be easily forgotten by a young man. There stood the orator and the man, and never since have I seen the two in such exquisite combination. The old Greek sculptor would have delighted to immortalize such a form in marble.

Whispering to a tall white brother beside me (the audience was half white) I asked: "Who, sir, is that man speaking?" "That man? That man is Frederick Douglass." Then looking down upon me with an expression of mingled pity and surprise in his face, he said: "Why, don't you know Fred Douglass?" I need not say that that question brought to my mind feelings of pride not altogether unmixed with humiliation.

As the old orator swept on, however, in his own inimitable style, sprinkling his remarks with genuine original wit I forgot everything else around me. His voice, a heavy barytone, or rendered a little heavier than usual by a slight hoarseness contracted in previous speaking, could be distinctly heard in that historic but most wretched of auditoriums. I was particularly struck with his perfect ease and naturalness, a seemingly childlike unconsciousness of his surroundings, while, like a master of his art, as he was, he swayed the feelings of that surging multitude. In the most impassioned portions of his speech, however, it was evident to the thoughtful observer that there was in the man immense reserved force which on momentous occasions might be used with startling effect.

At first I had entered the hall to remain but a few minutes, and, consequently, had taken my stand just inside the door. How long I did remain I cannot tell, but it was until the speaker finished, at which time I found myself half way up towards the rostrum in the midst of that thickly standing audience. Such was my first sight and impression of one of the world's great orators, and beyond comparison the greatest man of the race yet produced on this continent.

His splendid physique, so often admired, was well in keeping with the strength and grasp of his masterly mind. Without the privilege of a day's instruction in the schoolroom, he acquired a fund of useful knowledge that would put to shame the meager attainments of many a college graduate. His speeches and writing are models of a pure English style, and are characterized by simplicity, clearness, directness, force, and elegance.

Many of the interesting facts and incidents in the life of this great man are already well known—his escape from slavery, his arrival in the North, his early marriage, his settling down to work at his trade in New Bedford, his first speech in an anti-slavery convention, that drew attention to his wonderful powers of oratory, and led to his employment by the Anti-slavery Bureau to lecture through the North on the most unpopular question that up to that time had been presented to the American people, his rise as an orator, his trip to England and its magical effects on the English people, his return to this country, and the purchase of his freedom, to relieve him of the apprehension of being seized and taken back into slavery, his editorship of the North Star, his services to the government during the war in the raising of troops, his securing of pay for the black soldiers equal to that of the whites, the editorship immediately after the war of the New National Era, his popularity as a lyceum lecturer, his mission to San Domingo under Grant, his marshalship of the District of Columbia under Hayes, his ministry to Santo Domingo. These are some of the experiences which came into that eventful life.

If I were asked to sum up in a word what made Frederick Douglass great, I should say a noble purpose, fixed and unchangeable, a purpose to render to mankind the largest possible service. Verily he has served us well, faithfully, unselfishly, and now, full of years and full of honors, loaded with such distinctions as this poor world has to give, he dies, dies as he lived, a brave, strong, good man. No more shall we behold that manly form. No more shall we listen to those eloquent lips upon which for over fifty years so many thousands have hung with rapture, those eloquent lips that made his name famous in two hemispheres, and will surely keep it so long as freedom has a history. God grant that the mantle of this old hero may fall upon a worthy successor! God grant that our young men, contemplating his life and emulating his example, may be lifted up to a higher conception of life, of duty, of responsibility, of usefulness!

INCIDENT IN THE LIFE OF FREDERICK DOUGLASS

Long after the Civil War, Mr. Douglass once told the following story of his life to the pupils of a colored school in Talbot County, Maryland, the county in which he was born:

"I once knew a little colored boy whose father and mother died when he was six years old. He was a slave and had no one to care for him. He slept on a dirt floor in a hovel and in cold weather would crawl into a meal bag, headforemost, and leave his feet in the ashes to keep them warm. Often he would roast an ear of corn and eat it to satisfy his hunger, and many times has he crawled under the barn or stable and secured eggs, which he would roast in the fire and eat.

"This boy did not wear pants as you do, only a tow linen shirt. Schools were unknown to him, and he learned to spell from an old Webster's spelling book, and to read and write from posters on cellars and barn doors, while boys and men would help him. He would then preach and speak, and soon became well known. He finally held several high positions and accumulated some wealth. He wore broadcloth and did not have to divide crumbs with the dogs under the table. That boy was Frederick Douglass.

"What was possible for me is possible for you. Do not think because you are colored you can not accomplish anything. Strive earnestly to add to your knowledge. So long as you remain in ignorance, so long will you fail to command the respect of your fellow men."

ANIMAL LIFE IN THE CONGO

WILLIAM HENRY SHEPPARD

At daybreak Monday morning we had finished our breakfast by candle light and with staff in hand we marched northeast for Lukunga.

In two days we sighted the Mission Compound. Word had reached the missionaries (A.B.M.U.) that foreigners were approaching, and they came out to meet and greet us. We were soon hurried into their cool and comfortable mud houses. Our faithful cook was dismissed, for we were to take our meals with the missionaries.

Mr. Hoste, who is at the head of this station, came into our room and mentioned that the numerous spiders, half the size of your hand, on the walls were harmless. "But," said he, as he raised his hand and pointed to a hole over the door, "there is a nest of scorpions; you must be careful in moving in or out, for they will spring upon you."

Well, you ought to have seen us dodging in and out that door. After supper, not discrediting the veracity of the gentleman, we set to work, and for an hour we spoiled the walls by smashing spiders with slippers.

The next morning the mission station was excited over the loss of their only donkey. The donkey had been feeding in the field and a boa-constrictor had captured him, squeezed him into pulp, dragged him a hundred yards down to the river bank, and was preparing to swallow him. The missionaries, all with guns, took aim and fired, killing the twenty-five-foot boa-constrictor. The boa was turned over to the natives and they had a great feast. The missionaries told us many tales about how the boa-constrictor would come by night and steal away their goats, hogs, and dogs.

The sand around Lukunga is a hot-bed for miniature fleas, or "jiggers." The second day of our stay at Lukunga our feet had swollen and itched terribly, and on examination we found that these "jiggers" had entered under our toe nails and had grown to the size of a pea. A native was called and with a small sharpened stick they were cut out. We saw natives with toes and fingers eaten entirely off by these pests. Mr. Hoste told us to keep our toes well greased with palm oil. We followed his instructions, but grease with sand and sun made our socks rather "heavy."

The native church here is very strong spiritually. The church bell, a real big brass bell, begins to ring at 8 A. M. and continues for an hour. The natives in the neighborhood come teeming by every trail, take their seats quietly, and listen attentively to the preaching of God's word. No excitement, no shouting, but an intelligent interest shown by looking and listening from start to finish.

In the evening you can hear from every quarter our hymns sung by the natives in their own language. They are having their family devotions before retiring.

Our second day's march brought us to a large river. Our loads and men were ferried over in canoes. Mr. Lapsley and I decided to swim it, and so we jumped in and struck out for the opposite shore. On landing we were told by a native watchman that we had done a very daring thing. He explained with much excitement and many gestures that the river was filled with crocodiles, and that he did not expect to see us land alive on his side. We camped on the top of the hill overlooking N'Kissy and the wild rushing Congo Rapids. It was in one of these whirlpools that young Pocock, Stanley's last survivor, perished.

In the "Pool" we saw many hippopotami, and longed to go out in a canoe and shoot one, but being warned of the danger from the hippopotami and also of the treacherous current of the Congo River, which might take us over the rapids and to death, we were afraid to venture. A native Bateke fisherman, just a few days before our arrival, had been crushed in his canoe by a bull-hippopotamus. Many stories of hippopotami horrors were told us.

One day Chief N'Galiama with his attendant came to the mission and told Dr. Simms that the people in the village were very hungry and to see if it were possible for him to get some meat to eat.

Dr. Simms called me and explained how the people were on the verge of a famine and if I could kill them a hippopotamus it would help greatly. He continued to explain that the meat and hide would be dried by the people and, using but a little at each meal, would last them a long time. Dr. Simms mentioned that he had never hunted, but he knew where the game was. He said, "I will give you a native guide, you go with him around the first cataract about two miles from here and you will find the hippopotami." I was delighted at the idea, and being anxious to use my "Martini Henry" rifle and to help the hungry people, I consented to go. In an hour and a half we had walked around the rapids, across the big boulders, and right before us were at least a dozen big hippopotami. Some were frightened, ducked their heads and made off; others showed signs of fight and defiance.

At about fifty yards distant I raised my rifle and let fly at one of the exposed heads. My guide told me that the hippopotamus was shot and killed. In a few minutes another head appeared above the surface of the water and again taking aim I fired with the same result. The guide, who was a subject of the Chief N'Galiama, sprang upon a big boulder and cried to me to look at the big bubbles which were appearing on the water; then explained in detail that the hippopotami had drowned and would rise to the top of the water within an hour.

The guide asked to go to a fishing camp nearby and call some men to secure the hippopotami when they rose, or else they would go out with the current and over the rapids. In a very short time about fifty men, bringing native rope with them, were on the scene and truly, as the guide had said, up came the first hippopotamus, his big back showing first. A number of the men were off swimming with the long rope which was tied to the hippopotamus' foot. A signal was given and every man did his best. No sooner had we secured the one near shore than there was a wild shout to untie and hasten for the other. These two were securely tied by their feet and big boulders were rolled on the rope to keep them from drifting out into the current.

The short tails of both of them were cut off and we started home. We reported to Dr. Simms that we had about four or five tons of meat down on the river bank. The native town ran wild with delight. Many natives came to examine my gun which had sent the big bullets crashing through the brain of the hippopotami. Early the next morning N'Galiama sent his son Nzelie with a long caravan of men to complete the work. They leaped upon the backs of the hippopotami, wrestled with each other for a while, and then with knives and axes fell to work. The missionaries enjoyed a hippopotamus steak that day also.

Before the chickens began to crow for dawn I was alarmed by a band of big, broad-headed, determined driver ants. They filled the cabin, the bed, the yard. There were millions. They were in my head, my eyes, my nose, and pulling at my toes. When I found it was not a dream, I didn't tarry long.

Some of our native boys came with torches of fire to my rescue. They are the largest and the most ferocious ant we know anything about. In an incredibly short space of time they can kill any goat, chicken, duck, hog or dog on the place. In a few hours there is not a rat, mouse, snake, centipede, spider, or scorpion in your house, as they are chased, killed and carried away. We built a fire and slept inside of the circle until day.

We scraped the acquaintance of these soldier ants by being severely bitten and stung. They are near the size of a wasp and use both ends with splendid effect. They live deep down in the ground and come out of a smoothly cut hole, following each other single file, and when they reach a damp spot in the forest and hear the white ants cutting away on the fallen leaves, the leader stops until all the soldiers have caught up. A circle is formed, a peculiar hissing is the order to raid, and down under the leaves they dart, and in a few minutes they come out with their pinchers filled with white ants. The line, without the least excitement, is again formed and they march back home stepping high with their prey.

The small White Ants have a blue head and a white, soft body and are everywhere in the ground and on the surface. They live by eating dead wood and leaves.

We got rid of the driver ants by keeping up a big fire in their cave for a week. We dug up the homes of the big black ants and they moved off. But there was no way possible to rid the place of the billions of white ants. They ate our dry goods boxes, our books, our trunks, our beds, shoes, hats and clothing. The natives make holes in the ground, entrapping the ants, and use them for food.

The dogs look like ordinary curs, with but little hair on them, and they never bark or bite. I asked the people to explain why their dogs didn't bark. So they told me that once they did bark, but long ago the dogs and leopards had a big fight, the dogs whipped the leopards, and after that the leopards were very mad, so the mothers of the little dogs told them not to bark any more, and they hadn't barked since.

The natives tie wooden bells around their dogs to know where they are. Every man knows the sound of his bell just as we would know the bark of our dog.

There are many, many kinds of birds of the air, all known and called by name, and the food they eat, their mode of building nests, etc., were familiar to the people. They knew the customs and habits of the elephant, hippopotamus, buffalo, leopard, hyena, jackal, wildcat, monkey, mouse, and every animal which roams the great forest and plain,—from the thirty-foot boa-constrictor to a tiny tulu their names and nature were well known.

The little children could tell you the native names of all insects, such as caterpillars, crickets, cockroaches, grasshoppers, locusts, mantis, honey bees, bumble bees, wasps, hornets, yellow jackets, goliath beetles, stage beetles, ants, etc.

The many species of fish, eels and terrapins were on the end of their tongues, and these were all gathered and used for food. All the trees of the forest and plain, the flowers, fruits, nuts and berries were known and named. Roots which are good for all maladies were not only known to the medicine man, but the common people knew them also.

CO-OPERATION AND THE LATIN CLASS

LILLIAN B. WITTEN

The few minutes that intervened between the devotionals and the beginning of the first period were always eagerly seized by the Senior class in the L—— high school for those last furious attempts at learning the date of the battle of Marathon, the duties of the President of the United States, and other pieces of information that the faculty set so much store by.

Bored indifference was the sole notice they gave to the antics of the freshmen boys who were trying to get a Webster's unabridged dictionary on the floor of the aisle without attracting the attention of the guardian of the room.

One little group of seniors was especially busy, cooperatively busy one might say. This was one of the overflow divisions of eight students which made up a class in Virgil. In all of the athletics of their three years in school they had been taught the value of team work and coöperation. One bright student had conceived the idea of bringing this same team work into the Virgil class. It worked beautifully. Sixty lines of Virgil was their customary assignment. Sixty lines divided among eight students, as everybody could see, was about eight lines per student. Each pupil had his number and studied correspondingly: number one translated the first seven lines with great care, number two the second seven, et cetera down the line. Then during the study period which preceded the Latin recitation each one translated his lines for the benefit of the other seven, while they attentively followed his translation with the Latin text.

Busy over those vindictive lines in which Queen Dido, spurned by Aeneas, pronounces a curse upon his head and all his generation, the eight seniors on this particular morning translated one for the other, "Hate, with a never-ceasing hate." All of the savage beauty of the lines was lost on them, floundering in the maze of ablatives, subjunctives and the like. But they managed between them all to make out some sort of translation.

The composition work lent itself to team work much more effectively. There were ten sentences given them each day to be translated from English into Latin. They were divided among the eight in the same manner as the Virgil, each one taking turns in doing the two extra sentences. Passed around from one to the other and carefully copied they made up a carefully done composition lesson. The beauty of it was that the Latin teacher called upon them to put these sentences upon the board, each one being given a different sentence. Thus the similarity of the work could not be a subject of unpleasant comment by the teacher who never presumed to collect the notebooks.

The gong sounded for second period; noise and bustle commenced, the Virgil class made for the Latin recitation room with all the enthusiasm of prepared lessons. Time dragged today of all days, the day of the annual football game between the Juniors and the Seniors, so much more vivid than the wanderings of Aeneas. Red and orange, the colors of the Senior and Junior classes respectively, were everywhere conspicuous.

But lessons had to be gotten through somehow so with open books, making the final attempt to gather up loose ends in the translation, they waited for the recitation to commence. Miss Rhodes, the young Latin teacher, had observed the class during the three weeks of the new term. She had noted the fact that none of the class excelled the others, that all of them sometimes made brilliant recitations, all sometimes stumbled through passages in a way to cause the long deceased Virgil to blush with shame. The students could have explained that if she would always call upon them for the particular seven lines which had been their portion they could always be brilliant. However, they maintained a wise and discreet silence. Scientific observation and analysis is never wasted, however.

"Will the class please pass their Latin sentences to me?" Miss Rhodes requested at the beginning of the hour.

Eight pairs of eyes were instantly fixed on her in amazed consternation. Eight pairs of unwilling hands fumbled among papers and slowly gave up the one paper, which was the exact duplicate of every other paper. "Hurry, please, class. You may now write your translations of today's lesson for twenty minutes."

The clock ticked, eight industrious students concentrated and slaved over Dido's curse. Translations which sounded plausible enough when orally stumbled through did not look well when written. In the meantime Miss Rhodes looked through the sentences which they had given her. Her suspicions were confirmed. The class, unaware that they were harming only themselves, were daily copying their sentences from each other. Stolen glances at the young and pretty teacher informed the students that her mouth had tightened, her chin had suddenly become terrifyingly firm. After an eternity had passed the period came to an end.

"Class is dismissed. Please reassemble in this room this afternoon at 2.30," Miss Rhodes succinctly stated. Did they hear aright? Why, this afternoon was the afternoon of the game. It was incredible. Eight seniors and one of them the crack halfback of the senior team, not to be at their own game. It was not to be dreamed of. In vain they protested.

"If you expect to graduate, you will be here at 2.30. Cheaters deserve no consideration."

Half past two found the eight sad and wiser seniors again in the Latin room. Again they applied themselves to translating Latin into English, English into Latin, while in the distance they could hear the shouts of the football fans. The hours ticked by. The game was over, the Juniors winners in one of the closest games of years over the Seniors, who lost because of the absence of their halfback who sat translating Latin, failing his class in their need. He would never live down the shame.

Just before dismissing this extra session of the class, Miss Rhodes quietly said, "Let me tell you from experience that the ability to make a good bluff is a rare gift. Good bluffs are always founded on consistent hard work."

Slowly and sadly the Virgil class passed out of the room; realizing that the days of coöperative Virgil were relegated to the dim, suffering past.

THE BAND OF GIDEON

JOSEPH S. COTTER

The Band of Gideon roam the sky,
The howling wind is their war-cry,
The thunder's roll is their trump's peal,
And the lightning's flash their vengeful steel.
Each black cloud
Is a fiery steed.
And they cry aloud
With each strong deed,"
The sword of the Lord and Gideon."

And men below rear temples high
And mock their God with reasons why,
And live, in arrogance, sin and shame,
And rape their souls for the world's good name.
Each black cloud
Is a fiery steed.
And they cry aloud
With each strong deed,"
The sword of the Lord and Gideon."

The band of Gideon roam the sky
And view the earth with baleful eye;
In holy wrath they scourge the land
With earthquake, storm and burning brand.
Each black cloud
Is a fiery steed.
And they cry aloud
With each strong deed,
"The sword of the Lord and Gideon."

The lightnings flash and the thunders roll,
And "Lord have mercy on my soul,
"Cry men as they fall on the stricken sod,
In agony searching for their God.
Each black cloud
Is a fiery steed.
And they cry aloud
With each strong deed,
"The sword of the Lord and Gideon."

And men repent and then forget
That heavenly wrath they ever met,
The band of Gideon yet will come
And strike their tongues of blasphemy dumb.
Each black cloud
Is a fiery steed.
And they cry aloud
With each strong deed,
"The sword of the Lord and Gideon."

THE HOME OF THE COLORED GIRL BEAUTIFUL

AZALIA HACKLEY

The Home of the Colored Girl Beautiful will reflect her. She will help her parents to buy a home that it may give her family more standing in the civic community. Taste and simplicity will rule, for the home will harmonize with the girl. If her parents are not particular about the trifles in the way of curtains, fences, and yards, then it must be her special task to make the home represent the beautiful in her, the God, for all that is beautiful and good comes from God.

Windows generally express the character of the occupants of a house. The day has passed when soiled or ragged lace curtains are tolerated. The cheaper simpler scrims and cheese cloths which are easily laundered are now used by the best people.

The Colored Girl Beautiful will study the possibilities of her home and will attempt to secure the restful effects for the eye. Too much furniture is bad taste. The less one has, the cleaner houses may be kept.

The ornate heavy furniture and the upholstered parlor sets are passing away because they are no longer considered good taste, besides they are too heavy for cleanliness and are harmful to the health of women who do their own work.

Furniture of less expensive model, with simple lines and of less weight is being selected. This may be paid for in cash instead of "on time," as has been the custom of many people in smaller towns and in the country districts.

The furniture sold by the payment houses always shows its source in its heaviness and shininess.

The wall paper should be selected as one would select a color for clothes, to harmonize with the color of the skin in all lights, and for service. Color schemes in decoration are being followed and we have no more stuffy parlors, often closed for days. Instead we have living rooms, with cleanable furniture, strong but light, entirely suitable for winter, and cool in summer. No one has a parlor now-a-days. The best room is generally a living room for the whole family. No more do we see enlarged pictures which good taste demands should be placed in bedrooms and private sitting rooms. The ten-cent stores have done a great deal of good in educating the poor, white and black alike. These stores have everywhere sold small brown art prints of many of the great paintings, to take the place of the gaudy dust-laden chromos and family pictures.

Pictures are hung low that they may be thoroughly dusted, as well as to give a near view of the subject.

Expensive carpets are also things of the past. Painted and stained floors with light weight rugs are more generally used. These may be cleaned and handled without giving the backache to women. Many colored girls boast of having painted their own floors and woodwork. Much of this has been learned in the boarding school.

A tawdry home expresses its mistress as do her clothes. Next to the kitchen a fully equipped bath room is now the most important room in the house. Health and sanitation are the topics of the hour and a colored girl should know how to put a washer on a faucet as well as her father or brother.

A house without books is indeed an unfurnished home. Good books are the fad now. They are everywhere in evidence in the up-to-date colored home. They are exhibited almost as hand-painted china was. In every inventory or collection one finds a Bible, a dictionary, and an atlas.

The times are changing and the colored people are changing with the times. Cleanliness and health are the watchwords, and "Order" is Heaven's first law.

THE KNIGHTING OF DONALD

LILLIAN B. WITTEN

"With spear drawn Sir Cedric rode steadily through the forest, while ever nearer and nearer came the dragon. Swift and sudden was the onslaught and great was the struggle, until finally Sir Cedric dismounted from his black charger and stood victor over the huge monster who had committed so many depredations against the country side."

Slowly and lingeringly Donald closed the book. The many-branched tree under which he lay changed into a grey stone castle with moat and drawbridge upon which through the day armored knights on prancing steeds rode from castle to village, always on missions of good to the towns and hamlets. Never did Donald tire of reading about Arthur, Galahad, Merlin and the others, but Launcelot, the Bold, was his favorite knight. As he read of their deeds his black eyes flashed, his nervous slim body quivered, the deep rich red flooded his brown cheeks. He was one of them, took part in their tournaments, rescued the lovely ladies and overcame wicked monsters for his king.

Of all the stories a never-to-be-forgotten one was of a little boy like himself who lived in a small cottage near a castle which harbored many knights. This little boy idolized them even as Donald did. One day as the knights were returning from a strenuous day's work, one, weary and worn, stopped at the cottage and asked for a drink of water. Eagerly the boy ran, filled his cup at the brimming spring, and gave it to the knight.

"Thank you, my little boy," smiled the man. "Already you are a knight for you have learned the lesson of service."

How Donald envied the boy. To serve a knight, he dreamed, even to see one. Would he had lived in the olden times when knighthood was in flower. But having been born centuries too late he tried in every way to live as the knights had lived. Daily he exercised, practiced physical feats, restrained himself from over indulgence, following out the program of those who would be knights. With shining eyes he would often repeat his motto, the motto of Arthur's knights: "Live pure, speak the truth, right the wrong, follow the Christ."

Thus dreaming Donald grew and everybody loved him. Dreamer though he was, he ever kept before him the ideal of service. Tense with interest in the exploits of the black knight, he was often tempted not to answer when his mother called him from his reading to go on errands. Only a second, however, would temptation last. Launcelot could never approve of a boy who acted dishonestly.

Working, playing, and dreaming, Donald grew into a lovable boy, adept in all of the sports of boyhood and with the manners of a prince. He had reached the last year in grammar school, the graduating class. Already the obligations of maturity were forcing themselves upon the boys and girls. They, for the first time in their school career, were an organized group. They were going to elect officers, dignified officers. Nominations had been many and enthusiasm surged around the youthful candidates, but the choice for president had narrowed itself down between Donald and a laughing-eyed girl with crinkly black hair. As usual there were more girls in the class than boys, but while the boys stood solidly as one behind the masculine candidate, there were a few girls who put their trust in manly courage rather than feminine charm and were disposed to break loose from the suffragette camp. Public opinion thus gave the election to Donald.

As the time for election drew near, the interest became more intense and the various camps campaigned vigorously, each striving to gain the majority vote. One day as the school was assembling in their usual room they were stopped by the sight of their principal questioning one of the members of the class.

"But this is your knife, isn't it?" sternly inquired the principal.

"Yes, sir," responded John, a trustworthy boy, the son of a widowed mother whom he helped by working after school hours.

"Mr. Starks found this knife underneath his broken window last night. It had evidently been dropped by the boy who, in climbing out of his cherry tree, accidentally smashed the window. You know that I announced last week that the next boy who was caught trespassing upon Mr. Starks' property would be suspended from school for the rest of the year. I am disappointed in you, John. This does not sound like you. Did you drop this knife last night?"

"No, sir," responded John.

"No? Well, speak up. Who had the knife?"

"I can't say, sir."

"But you must. This is a serious matter. One of the rules of the school has been broken." Then looking nervously around the room of girls and boys, the principal commanded: "Will the boy who dropped this knife last night speak, or shall I be forced to find out the culprit for myself?"

There was no answer. Every boy stood taut, his eyes steadfastly before him in the thick silence that followed.

"Very well," snapped the principal. "John, who had the knife yesterday?"

"I cannot say, sir," responded John unwillingly.

"You may do one of two things, either you will tell the name of the boy to whom you lent the knife or you may be suspended from school for the rest of the year."

The silence was more intense. One, two, three minutes passed.

"You are dismissed," said the principal.

Slowly John left the room. Three days passed. John's mother, much disturbed, bewailed the fact that he would lose this year out of his school life and, perhaps, would not have the opportunity of going again. John thought of the responsibility toward his mother and then of that toward the boy whose fault he was concealing. Was he doing right or was he doing the easiest thing in not telling?

On the fourth day John sought the principal. "If it is necessary to tell the name of the boy who had my knife before I can return to school, I will tell," he anxiously said.

"It certainly is necessary."

And John told.

There was great excitement in the graduating class. The traditions of centuries had been broken. One of their number had become a tattler. John resumed his school work, systematically and obviously shunned by the other boys.

But Donald reflected over the incident. "After all," he thought, "John did the bravest thing. It would have been easier to appear heroic and to sacrifice his mother for the sake of a boy who needed to be punished."

The next day Donald sought John, accompanied him to school, and showed the class that he regarded John as a hero instead of a tell-tale.

The boys divided into two camps, some following Donald's example, and others loudly denouncing him.

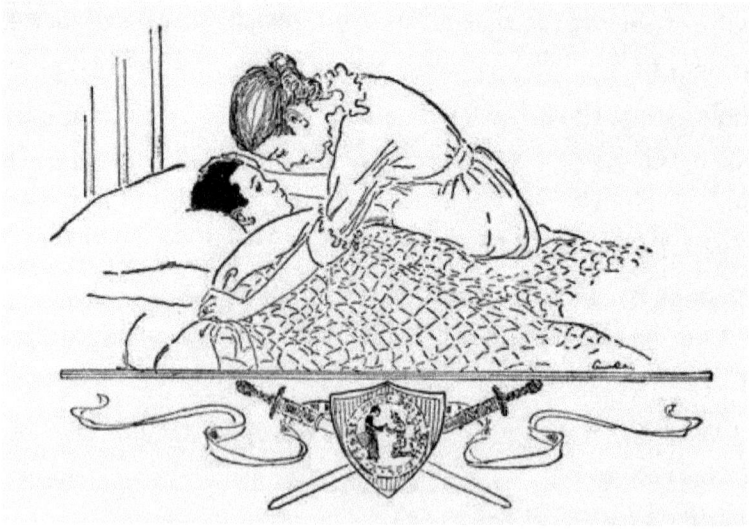

Donald's sponsorship of John cost him the presidential election just as he had foreseen, but he knew that he had lived up to the best within him and he was satisfied.

As he climbed into bed at the end of the day upon which he had been defeated and yet had gained a great victory, his mother tucked the covers closely around him, kissed him good-night, and lowered the light. Then she bent over him again and kissed him once more and whispered,

"My brave little knight."

A NEGRO EXPLORER AT THE NORTH POLE

MATTHEW A. HENSON

"Matthew A. Henson, my Negro assistant, has been with me in one capacity or another since my second trip to Nicaragua in 1887. I have taken him on each and all of my expeditions, except the first, and also without exception on each of my farthest sledge trips. This position I have given him primarily because of his adaptability and fitness for the work and secondly on account of his loyalty. He is a better dog driver and can handle a sledge better than any man living, except some of the best Esquimo hunters themselves.

"Robert E. Peary, Rear Admiral, U. S. N."

Exactly 40° below zero when we pushed the sledges up to the curled-up dogs and started them off over rough ice covered with deep soft snow. It was like walking in loose granulated sugar. Indeed I might compare the snow of the Arctic to the granules of sugar, without their saccharine sweetness, but with freezing cold instead; you cannot make snowballs of it, for it is too thoroughly congealed, and when it is packed by the wind it is almost as solid as ice. It is from the packed snow that the blocks used to form the igloo-walls are cut.

At the end of four hours, we came to the igloo where the Captain and his boys were sleeping the sleep of utter exhaustion. In order not to interrupt the Captain's rest, we built another igloo and unloaded his sledge, and distributed the greater part of the load among the sledges of the party. The Captain, on awakening, told us that the journey we had completed on that day had been made by him under the most trying conditions, and that it had taken him fourteen hours to do it. We were able to make better time because we had his trail to follow, and, therefore, the necessity of finding the easiest way was avoided. That was the object of the scout or pioneer party and Captain Bartlett had done practically all of it up to the time he turned back at 87° 48′ north.

March 29, 1909: You have undoubtedly taken into consideration the pangs of hunger and of cold that you know assailed us, going Poleward; but have you ever considered that we were thirsty for water to drink or hungry for fat? To eat snow to quench our thirsts would have been the height of folly, and as well as being thirsty, we were continually assailed by the pangs of a hunger that called for the fat, good, rich, oily, juicy fat that our systems craved and demanded.

Had we succumbed to the temptations of the thirst and eaten the snow, we would not be able to tell the tale of the conquest of the Pole; for the result of eating snow is death. True, the dogs licked up enough moisture to quench their thirsts, but we were not made of such stern stuff as they. Snow would have reduced our temperatures and we would quickly have fallen by the way. We had to wait until camp was made and the fire of alcohol started before we had a chance, and it was with hot tea that we quenched our thirsts. The hunger for fat was not appeased; a dog or two was killed, but his carcass went to the Esquimos and the entrails were fed to the rest of the pack.

April 1, the Farthest North of Bartlett: I knew at this time that he was to go back, and that I was to continue, so I had no misgivings and neither had he. He was ready and anxious to take the back-trail. His five marches were up and he was glad of it, and he was told that in the morning he must turn back and knit the trail together, so that the main column could return over a beaten path.

He swept his little party together and at three P. M., with a cheery "Good-by! Good Luck!" he was off. His Esquimo boys, attempting English, too, gave us their "Good-bys."

The Captain had gone. Commander Peary and I were alone (save for the four Esquimos), the same we had been with so often in the past years, and as we looked at each other we realized our position and we knew without speaking that the time had come for us to demonstrate that we were the men who it had been ordained, should unlock the door which held the mystery of the Arctic. Without an instant's hesitation, the order to push on was given, and we started off in the trail made by the Captain to cover the Farthest North he had made and to push on over one hundred and thirty miles to our final destination.

Day and night were the same. My thoughts were on the going and getting forward, and on nothing else. The wind was from the southeast, and seemed to push on, and the sun was at our backs, a ball of livid fire, rolling his way above the horizon in never-ending day.

With my proven ability in gauging distances, Commander Peary was ready to take the reckoning as I made it and he did not resort to solar observations until we were within a hand's grasp of the Pole.

The memory of those last five marches, from the Farthest North of Captain Bartlett to the arrival of our party at the Pole, is a memory of toil, fatigue, and exhaustion, but we were urged on and encouraged by our relentless commander, who was himself being scourged by the final lashings of the dominating influence that had controlled his life. From the land to 87° 48′ north, Commander Peary had had the best of the going, for he had brought up the rear and had utilized the trail made by the preceding parties, and thus he had kept himself in the best of condition for the time when he made the spurt that brought him to the end of the race. From 87° 48′ north, he kept in the lead and did his work in such a way as to convince me that he was still as good a man as he had ever been. We marched and marched, falling down in our tracks repeatedly, until it was impossible to go on. We were forced to camp, in spite of the impatience of the Commander, who found himself unable to rest, and who only waited long enough for us to relax into sound sleep, when he would wake us up and start us off again. I do not believe that he slept for one hour from April 2 until after he had loaded us up and ordered us to go back over our old trail, and I often think that from the instant when the order to return was given until the land was again sighted, he was in a continual daze.

Onward we forced our weary way. Commander Peary took his sights from the time our chronometer-watches gave, and I, knowing that we had kept on going in practically a straight line, was sure that we had more than covered the necessary distance to insure our arrival at the top of the earth.

It was during the march of the 3d of April that I endured an instant of hideous horror. We were crossing a lane of moving ice. Commander Peary was in the lead setting the pace, and a half hour later the four boys and myself followed in single file. They had all gone before, and I was standing and pushing at the upstanders of my sledge, when the block of ice I was using as a support slipped from underneath my feet, and before I knew it the sledge was out of my grasp, and I was floundering in the water of the lead. I did the best I could. I tore my hood from off my head and struggled frantically. My hands were gloved and I could not take hold of the ice, but before I could give the "Grand Hailing Sigh of Distress," faithful old Ootah had grabbed me by the nape of the neck, the same as he would have grabbed a dog, and with one hand he pulled me out of the water, and with the other hurried the team across.

He had saved my life, but I did not tell him so, for such occurrences are taken as part of the day's work, and the sledge he safeguarded was of much more importance, for it held, as part of its load, the Commander's sextant, the mercury, and the coils of piano-wire that were the essential portion of the scientific part of the expedition. My kamiks (boots of sealskin) were stripped off, and the congealed water was beaten out of my bearskin trousers, and with a dry pair of kamiks, we hurried on to overtake the column. When we caught up, we found the boys gathered around the Commander, doing their best to relieve him of his discomfort, for he had fallen into the water, also, and while he was not complaining, I was sure that his bath had not been any more voluntary than mine had been.

It was about ten or ten-thirty A. M., on the 7th of April, 1909, that the Commander gave the order to build a snow-shield to protect him from the flying drift of the surface-snow. I knew that he was about to take an observation, and while we worked I was nervously apprehensive, for I felt that the end of our journey had come. When we handed him the pan of mercury the hour was within a very few minutes of noon. Lying flat on his stomach, he took the elevation and made the notes on a piece of tissue-paper at his head. With sun-blinded eyes, he snapped shut the vernier (a graduated scale that subdivides the smallest divisions on the sector of the circular scale of the sextant) and with the resolute squaring of his jaws, I was sure that he was satisfied, and I was confident that the journey had ended.

The Commander gave the word, "We will plant the Stars and Stripes—*at the North Pole*!" and it was done; on the peak of a huge paleocrystic floeberg the glorious banner was unfurled to the breeze, and as it snapped and crackled with the wind, I felt a savage joy and exultation. Another world's accomplishment was done and finished, and as in the past, from the beginning of history, wherever the world's work was done by a white man, he had been accompanied by a colored man. From the building of the pyramids and the journey to the Cross, to the discovery of the North Pole, the Negro had been the faithful and constant companion of the Caucasian, and I felt all that it was possible for me to feel, that it was I, a lowly member of my race, who had been chosen by fate to represent it, at this, almost the last of the world's great work.

BENJAMIN BANNEKER

WILLIAM WELLS BROWN

Benjamin Banneker was born in the State of Maryland, in the year 1732, of pure African parentage; their blood never having been corrupted by the introduction of a drop of Anglo-Saxon. His father was a slave, and of course could do nothing towards the education of the child. The mother, however, being free, succeeded in purchasing the freedom of her husband, and they, with their son, settled on a few acres of land, where Benjamin remained during the lifetime of his parents. His entire schooling was gained from an obscure country school, established for the education of the children of free negroes; and these advantages were poor, for the boy appears to have finished studying before he arrived at his fifteenth year.

Although out of school, Banneker was still a student, and read with great care and attention such books as he could get. Mr. George Ellicott, a gentlemen of fortune and considerable literary taste, and who resided near to Benjamin, became interested in him, and lent him books from his large library. Among these books were three on Astronomy. A few old and imperfect astronomical instruments also found their way into the boy's hands, all of which he used with great benefit to his own mind.

Banneker took delight in the study of the languages, and soon mastered the Latin, Greek and German. He was also proficient in the French. The classics were not neglected by him, and the general literary knowledge which he possessed caused Mr. Ellicott to regard him as the most learned man in the town, and he never failed to introduce Banneker to his most distinguished guests.

About this time Benjamin turned his attention particularly to astronomy, and determined on making calculations for an almanac, and completed a set for the whole year. Encouraged by this attempt, he entered upon calculations for subsequent years, which, as well as the former, he began and finished without the least assistance from any person or books than those already mentioned; so that whatever merit is attached to his performance is exclusively his own.

He published an almanac in Philadelphia for the years 1792, '93, '94, and '95, which contained his calculations, exhibiting the different aspects of the planets, a table of the motions of the sun and moon, their risings and settings, and the courses of the bodies of the planetary system. By this time Banneker's acquirements had become generally known, and the best scholars in the country opened correspondence with him. Goddard & Angell, the well-known Baltimore publishers, engaged his pen for their establishment, and became the publishers of his almanacs.

He knew every branch of history, both natural and civil; he had read all the original historians of England, France, and was a great antiquarian. With such a fund of knowledge his conversation was equally interesting, instructive, and entertaining. Banneker was so favorably appreciated by the first families in Virginia, that in 1803 he was invited by Mr. Jefferson, then President of the United States, to visit him at Monticello, where the statesman had gone for recreation. But he was too infirm to undertake the journey. He died the following year, aged seventy-two. Like the golden sun that has sunk beneath the western horizon, but still throws upon the world, which he sustained and enlightened in his career, the reflected beams of his departed genius, his name can only perish with his language.

THE NEGRO RACE

CHARLES W. ANDERSON

As a race, we have done much, but we must not forget how much more there is still to do. To some extent we have been given opportunity, but we must not cease to remember that no race can be given relative rank—it must win equality of rating for itself. Hence, we must not only acquire education, but character as well. It is not only necessary that we should speak well, but it is more necessary that we should speak the truth.

PAUL CUFFE

JOHN W. CROMWELL

Paul Cuffe was born in 1759 on the island of Cuttyhunk, near New Bedford, Massachusetts. There were four sons and six daughters of John Cuffe who had been stolen from Africa, and Ruth, a woman of Indian extraction. Paul, the youngest son, lacked the advantage of an early education, but he supplied the deficiency by his personal efforts and learned not only to read and write with facility, but made such proficiency in the art of navigation as to become a skillful seaman and the instructor of both whites and blacks in the same art.

His father, who had obtained his freedom and bought a farm of one hundred acres, died when Paul was about fourteen. When he was sixteen, Paul began the life of a sailor. On his third voyage he was captured by a British brig and was for three months a prisoner of war. On his release he planned to go into business on his own account. With the aid of an elder brother, David Cuffe, an open boat was built in which they went to sea; but this brother on the first intimation of danger gave up the venture and Paul was forced to undertake the work single-handed and alone, which was a sore disappointment. On his second attempt he lost all he had.

Before the close of the Revolutionary War, Paul refused to pay a personal tax, on the ground that free colored people did not enjoy the rights and privileges of citizenship. After considerable delay, and an appeal to the courts, he paid the tax under protest. He then petitioned to the legislature which finally agreed to his contention. His efforts are the first of which there is any record of a citizen of African descent making a successful appeal in behalf of his civil rights. On reaching the age of twenty-five he married a woman of the same tribe as his mother, and for a while gave up life on the ocean wave; but the growth of his family led him back to his fond pursuit on the briny deep. As he was unable to purchase a boat, with the aid of his brother he built one from keel to gunwale and launched into the enterprise.

While on the way to a nearby island to consult his brother whom he had induced once more to venture forth with him, he was overtaken by pirates who robbed him of all he possessed. Again Paul returned home disappointed, though not discouraged. Once more he applied for assistance to his brother David and another boat was built. After securing a cargo, he met again with pirates, but he eluded them though he was compelled to return and repair his boat. These having been made, he began a successful career along the coast as far north as Newfoundland, to the south as far as Savannah and as distant as Gottenburg.

In carrying on this business, starting in the small way indicated, he owned at different times besides smaller boats, "The Ranger," a schooner of sixty or seventy tons, a half interest in a brig of 162 tons, the brig "Traveller," of 109 tons, the ship "Alpha," of 268 tons and three-fourths interest in a larger vessel.

A few noble incidents may illustrate his resourcefulness, difficulties and success over all obstacles. When engaged in the whaling business he was found with less than the customary outfit for effectually carrying on this work. The practice in such cases was for the other ships to loan the number of men needed. They denied this at first to Cuffe, but fair play prevailed and they gave him what was customary, with the result that of the seven whales captured, Paul's men secured five, and two of them fell by his own hand!

In 1795 he took a cargo to Norfolk, Virginia, and learning that corn could be bought at a decided advantage, he made a trip to the Nanticoke River, on the eastern shore of Maryland. Here his appearance as a black man commanding his own boat and with a crew of seven men all of his own complexion, alarmed the whites, who seemed to dread his presence there as the signal for a revolt on the part of their slaves. They opposed his landing, but the examination of his papers removed all doubts as to the regularity of his business, while his quiet dignity secured the respect of the leading white citizens. He had no difficulty after this in taking a cargo of three thousand bushels of corn, from which he realized a profit of $1000. On a second voyage he was equally successful.

Although without the privilege of attending a school when a boy, he endeavored to have his friends and neighbors open and maintain one for the colored and Indian children of the vicinity. Failing to secure their active coöperation, he built in 1797 a schoolhouse without their aid.

Because of his independent means and his skill as a mariner, he visited with little or no difficulty most of the larger cities of the country, held frequent conferences with the representative men of his race, and recommended the formation of societies for their mutual relief and physical betterment. Such societies he formed in Philadelphia and New York, and then having made ample preparation he sailed in 1811 for Africa in his brig "The Traveller," reaching Sierra Leone on the West Coast after a voyage of about two months.

Here he organized the Friendly Society of Sierra Leone and then went to Liverpool. Even here one of his characteristic traits manifested itself in taking with him to England for education a native of Sierra Leone.

While in England, Cuffe visited London twice and consulted such friends of the Negro as Granville Sharp, Thomas Clarkson and William Wilberforce! These men were all interested in a proposition to promote the settlement on the West Coast of Africa of the free people of color in America, many of whom had come into the domains of Great Britain as an outcome of the Revolutionary War. This opinion was at this period the prevailing sentiment of England respecting what was best for the Negro. Sir J. J. Crooks, a former governor of Sierra Leone, in alluding to its origin, says: "There is no doubt that the influence of their opinion was felt in America and that it led to emigration thence to Africa before Liberia was settled. Paul Cuffe, a man of color ... who was much interested in the promotion of the civil and religious liberty of his colored brethren in their native land, had been familiar with the ideas of these philanthropists, as well as with the movement in the same direction in England."[1]

[1]*History of Sierra Leone*, Dublin, 1903, p. 97

This explains Cuffe's visit to England and to Africa—a daring venture in those perilous days—and the formation of the Friendly Societies in Africa and in his own country, the United States.

When his special mission to England was concluded, he took out a cargo from Liverpool for Sierra Leone, after which he returned to America.

Before he made his next move, Cuffe consulted with the British Government in London and President Madison at Washington. But the strained relations between the two nations, as well as the financial condition of the United States at the time, made governmental coöperation impracticable if not impossible.

In 1815 he carried out the ideas long in his mind. In this year he sailed from Boston for Sierra Leone with thirty-eight free Negroes as settlers on the Black Continent. Only eight of these could pay their own expenses, but Cuffe, nevertheless, took out the entire party, landed them safe on the soil of their forefathers after a journey of fifty-five days and paid the expense for the outfit, transportation and maintenance of the remaining thirty, amounting to no less than twenty-five thousand dollars ($25,000), out of his own pocket. The colonists were cordially welcomed by the people of Sierra Leone, and each family received from thirty to forty acres from the Crown Government. He remained with the settlers two months and then returned home with the purpose of taking out another colony. Before, however, he could do so, and while preparations were being made for the second colony, he was taken ill. After a protracted illness he died September 7, 1817, in the fifty-ninth year of his age. At the time of his death he had no less than two thousand names of intending emigrants on his list awaiting transportation to Africa.

As to his personal characteristics: Paul Cuffe was "tall, well-formed and athletic, his deportment conciliating yet dignified and prepossessing. He was a member of the Society of Friends (Quakers) and became a minister among them.... He believed it to be his duty to sacrifice private interest, rather than engage in any enterprise, however lawful ... or however profitable, that had the slightest tendency to injure his fellow man. He would not deal in intoxicating liquors or in slaves."

THE BLACK FAIRY

FENTON JOHNSON

Little Annabelle was lying on the lawn, a volume of Grimm before her. Annabelle was nine years of age, the daughter of a colored lawyer, and the prettiest dark child in the village. She had long played in the fairyland of knowledge, and was far advanced for one of her years. A vivid imagination was her chief endowment, and her story creatures often became real flesh-and-blood creatures.

"I wonder," she said to herself that afternoon, "if there is any such thing as a colored fairy? Surely there must be, but in this book they're all white."

Closing the book, her eyes rested upon the landscape that rolled itself out lazily before her. The stalks in the cornfield bent and swayed, their tassels bowing to the breeze, until Annabelle could have easily sworn that those were Indian fairies. And beyond lay the woods, dark and mossy and cool, and there many a something mysterious could have sprung into being, for in the recess was a silvery pool where the children played barefooted. A summer mist like a thin veil hung over the scene, and the breeze whispered tales of far-away lands.

Hist! Something stirred in the hazel bush near her. Can I describe little Annabelle's amazement at finding in the bush a palace and a tall and dark-faced fairy before it?

"I am Amunophis, the Lily of Ethiopia," said the strange creature. "And I come to the children of the Seventh Veil."

She was black and regal, and her voice was soft and low and gentle like the Niger on a summer evening. Her dress was the wing of the sacred beetle, and whenever the wind stirred it played the dreamiest of music. Her feet were bound with golden sandals, and on her head was a crown of lotus leaves.

"And you're a fairy?" gasped Annabelle.

"Yes, I am a fairy, just as you wished me to be. I live in the tall grass many, many miles away, where a beautiful river called the Niger sleeps." And stretching herself beside Annabelle, on the lawn, the fairy began to whisper:

The Black Fairy

"I have lived there for over five thousand years. In the long ago a city rested there, and from that spot black men and women ruled the world. Great ships laden with spice and oil and wheat would come to its port, and would leave with wines and weapons of war and fine linens. Proud and great were the black kings of this land, their palaces were built of gold, and I was the Guardian of the City. But one night when I was visiting an Indian grove the barbarians from the North came down and destroyed our shrines and palaces and took our people up to Egypt. Oh, it was desolate, and I shed many tears, for I missed the busy hum of the market and the merry voices of the children.

"But come with me, little Annabelle, I will show you all this, the rich past of the Ethiopian."

She bade the little girl take hold of her hand and close her eyes, and wish herself in the wood behind the cornfield. Annabelle obeyed, and ere they knew it they were sitting beside the clear water in the pond.

"You should see the Niger," said the fairy. "It is still beautiful, but not as happy as in the old days. The white man's foot has been cooled by its water, and the white man's blossom is choking out the native flower." And she dropped a tear so beautiful the costliest pearl would seem worthless beside it.

"Ah! I did not come to weep," she continued, "but to show you the past."

So in a voice sweet and sad she sang an old African lullaby and dropped into the water a lotus leaf. A strange mist formed, and when it had disappeared she bade the little girl to look into the pool. Creeping up Annabelle peered into the glassy surface, and beheld a series of vividly colored pictures.

First she saw dark blacksmiths hammering in the primeval forests and giving fire and iron to all the world. Then she saw the gold of old Ghana and the bronzes of Benin. Then the black Ethiopians poured down upon Egypt and the lands and cities bowed and flamed. Next she saw a great city with pyramids and stately temples. It was night, and a crimson moon was in the sky. Red wine was flowing freely, and beautiful dusky maidens were dancing in a grove of palms. Old and young were intoxicated with the joy of living, and a sense of superiority could be easily traced in their faces and attitude. Presently red flame hissed everywhere, and the magnificence of remote ages soon crumbled into ash and dust. Persian soldiers ran to and fro conquering the band of defenders and severing the woman and children. Then came the Mohammedans and kingdom on kingdom arose, and with the splendor came ever more slavery.

The next picture was that of a group of fugitive slaves, forming the nucleus of three tribes, hurrying back to the wilderness of their fathers.

In houses built as protection against the heat the blacks dwelt, communing with the beauty of water and sky and open air. It was just between twilight and evening and their minstrels were chanting impromptu hymns to their gods of nature. And as she listened closely, Annabelle thought she caught traces of the sorrow songs in the weird pathetic strains of the African music mongers. From the East the warriors of the tribe came, bringing prisoners, whom they sold to white strangers from the West.

"It is the beginning," whispered the fairy, as a large Dutch vessel sailed westward. Twenty boys and girls bound with strong ropes were given to a miserable existence in the hatchway of the boat. Their captors were strange creatures, pale and yellow haired, who were destined to sell them as slaves in a country cold and wild, where the palm trees and the cocoanut never grew and men spoke a language without music. A light, airy creature, like an ancient goddess, flew before the craft guiding it in its course.

"That is I," said the fairy. "In that picture I am bringing your ancestors to America. It was my hope that in the new civilization I could build a race that would be strong enough to redeem their brothers. They have gone through great tribulations and trials, and have mingled with the blood of the fairer race; yet though not entirely Ethiopian they have not lost their identity. Prejudice is a furnace through which molten gold is poured. Heaven be merciful unto all races! There is one more picture—the greatest of all, but— farewell, little one, I am going."

"Going?" cried Annabelle. "Going? I want to see the last picture—and when will you return, fairy?"

"When the race has been redeemed. When the brotherhood of man has come into the world; and there is no longer a white civilization or a black civilization, but the civilization of all men. I belong to the world council of the fairies, and we are all colors and kinds. Why should not men be as charitable unto one another? When that glorious time comes I shall walk among you and be one of you, performing my deeds of magic and playing with the children of every nation, race and tribe. Then, Annabelle, you shall see the last picture—and the best."

Slowly she disappeared like a summer mist, leaving Annabelle amazed.

IT'S A LONG WAY

WILLIAM STANLEY BRAITHWAITE

It's a long way the sea-winds blow
Over the sea-plains blue,—
But longer far has my heart to go
Before its dreams come true.

It's work we must, and love we must,
And do the best we may,
And take the hope of dreams in trust
To keep us day by day.

It's a long way the sea-winds blow—
But somewhere lies a shore—
Thus down the tide of Time shall flow
My dreams forevermore.

NEGRO MUSIC THAT STIRRED FRANCE

EMMETT J. SCOTT

"You cannot defeat a singing nation," a keen-witted observer has said, in noting the victory spirit engendered by the martial music, the patriotic songs and the stirring melodies of hearth and home that have moved the souls of men to action on all the battlefields of history.

"Send me more singing regiments," cabled General Pershing, and Admiral Mayo sent frequent requests that a song leader organize singing on every battleship of the Atlantic Fleet.

Since "the morning stars sang together" in Scriptural narrative, music has exerted a profound influence upon mankind, be it in peace or in war, in gladness or in sorrow, or in the tender sentiment that makes for love of country, affection for kindred or the divine passion for "ye ladye fair." Music knows no land or clime, no season or circumstance, and no race, creed or clan. It speaks the language universal, and appeals to all peoples with a force irresistible and no training in ethics or science is necessary to reach the common ground that its philosophy instinctively creates in the human understanding.

The War Department was conscious of this and gave practical application to its theory that music makes a soldier "fit to fight" when it instituted, through the Commission on Training Camp Activities, a systematic program of musical instruction throughout the American Army at the home cantonments and followed up the work overseas. It was the belief that every man became a better warrior for freedom when his mind could be diverted from the dull routine of camp life by arousing his higher nature by song, and that he fared forth to battle with a stouter heart when his steps were attuned to the march by bands that drove out all fear of bodily danger and robbed "grim-visaged war" of its terrors. Skilled song leaders were detailed to the various camps and cantonments here and abroad, and bands galore were brought into service for inspiration and cheer.

The emotional nature of the Negro fitted him for this musical program. The colored American was a "close up" in every picture from the start to the finish and was a conspicuous figure in every scenario, playing with credit and distinction alike in melody or with the musket.

No instrumentality was more potent than music in off-setting the propaganda of the wily German agents, who sought to break down the loyalty of the Negro. The music he knew was intensely American—in sentiment and rhythm. It saturated his being—and all the blandishments of the enemy were powerless to sway him from the flag he loved. His grievances were overshadowed by the realization that the welfare of the nation was menaced and that his help was needed. American music harmonized with the innate patriotism of the race, and the majestic sweep of "The Star-Spangled Banner" or the sympathetic appeal of "My Country, 'Tis of Thee," were sufficient to counteract the sinister efforts of the missionaries of the Hohenzollerns to move him from his moorings.

No labor is ever so onerous that it can bar music from the soul of black folk. This race sings at work, at play and in every mood. Visitors to any army camp found the Negro doing musical "stunts" of some kind from reveille to taps—every hour, every minute of the day. All the time the trumpeters were not blowing out actual routine bugle calls, they were somewhere practicing them. Mouth-organs were going, concertinas were being drawn back and forth, and guitars, banjos, mandolins and whatnot were in use—playing all varieties of music, from the classic, like "Lucia," "Poet and Peasant," and "Il Trovatore" to the folksongs and the rollicking "Jazz." Music is indeed the chiefest outlet of the Negro's emotions, and the state of his soul can best be determined by the type of melody he pours forth.

Some writer has said that a handful of pipers at the head of a Scotch regiment could lead that regiment down the mouth of a cannon. It is not doubted that a Negro regiment could be made to duplicate the "Charge of the Light Brigade" at Balaklava—"into the mouth of hell," as Tennyson puts it—if one of their regimental bands should play—as none but a colored band can play—the vivacious strains of "There'll Be a Hot Time in the Old Town Tonight."

The Negro's love of home is an integral part of his nature, and is exemplified in the themes he plaintively crooned in camp on both sides of the ocean. Such melodies as "Carry Me Back to Old Virginia," "My Old Kentucky Home," "In the Evening by de Moonlight," and "Swanee River" recalled memories of the "old folks at home," and kept his patriotism alive, for he hoped to return to them some day and swell their hearts with pride by reason of the glorious record he made at the front.

The Negro is essentially religious, and his deep spiritual temperament is vividly illustrated by the joy he finds in "harmonizing" such ballads of ancient days as "Swing Low, Sweet Chariot," "Steal Away to Jesus," "Standin' in the Need of Prayer," "Every Time I Feel the Spirit," "I Wan' to be Ready," and "Roll, Jordan, Roll." The Negro is also an optimist, whether he styles himself by that high-sounding title or not, and the sincerity of his "make the best of it" disposition is noted in the fervor he puts into those uplifting gems, "Pack Up Your Troubles in Your Old Kit Bag and Smile, Smile, Smile," "There's a Long, Long Trail," "Keep the Home Fires Burning," and "Good-bye Broadway, Hello France."

Just as the Negro folk-songs—or songs of war, interpreted with the characteristic Negro flavor—stirred all France and gave poilu and populace a taste of the real American music, the marvelous "jazz bands" kept their feet patting and their shoulders "eagle-rocking" to its infectious motion. High officials are said to have been literally "carried away" with the "jazz" music furnished by the colored bands "over there" during the war. General Petain is said to have paid a visit, at the height of the hostilities, to a sector in which there were American troops and had "the time of his life" listening to a colored band playing the entrancing "jazz" music, with some Negro dance stunts in keeping with the spirit of the melodies. He warmly congratulated the colored leader upon the excellence of the work of his organization, and thanked him for the enjoyable entertainment that had been given him.

The stolid Briton is scarcely less susceptible to the "jazz" than his volatile French brother, for when another colored band from "The States" went to London to head a parade of American and English soldiers, and halted at Buckingham Palace, it is said that King George V and Queen Mary heard the lively airs with undisguised enthusiasm and were loath to have the players depart for the park where they were scheduled for a concert, with a dance engagement, under British military control, to follow. The colored bands scored heavily with the three great Allied Powers of Europe by rendering with a brilliant touch and matchless finish their national anthems, "God Save the Queen," "La Marseillaise" and the "Marcia Reale."

NOVEMBER 11, 1918

(This letter was written by a young first lieutenant (colored) in the 366th Infantry, Company L, 92nd Division, Cleveland, Ohio.)

November 11th.

My dearest Mother and Dad:

Well, folks, it's all over but the flowers. Yesterday it was war, hard, gruelling, hideous. Today it is peace.

This morning I formed my platoon in line in the woods behind the line. They didn't know why. They were just a bunch of tired, hard-bitten, mud-spattered, rough-and-tumble soldiers standing stoically at attention, equally ready to go over the top, rebuild a shell-torn road, or march to a rest billet. At 10:45 I gave the command: "Unload rifles!" They didn't know why and didn't particularly care. Then—"Unload pistols." And while they still stood rigid and motionless as graven images, I read the order declaring armistice and cessation of hostilities effective at 11 o'clock. The perfect discipline of these veteran soldiers held them still motionless, but I could see their eyes begin to shine and their muscles to quiver as the import of this miraculous message began to dawn on them.

The tension was fast straining their nerves to the breaking-point, so I dismissed them. You should have seen them! They yelled till they were hoarse. Some sang. Others, war-hardened veterans, who had faced the death hail of a machine-gun with a laugh, men who had gone through the horrors of artillery bombardments and had seen their fellows mangled and torn without a flinch, broke down and cried like babies.

Tonight something is wrong. The silence is almost uncanny. Not a shot—not even a single shell. Very faintly we can hear the mellow tones of the church bell in the little French town on the hill far to our rear. All day long it has been singing its song of joy and thanksgiving. It seems symbolical of the heart of France, which, today, is ringing.

I don't know when I'm coming home, but when I do, I want a big roast turkey, golden brown, new spuds swimming in butter and cranberry sauce.

Love,
JESSE.

SEA LYRIC

WILLIAM STANLEY BRAITHWAITE

Over the seas to-night, love,
Over the darksome deeps,
Over the seas to-night, love,
Slowly my vessel creeps.

Over the seas to-night, love,
Waking the sleeping foam—
Sailing away from thee, love,
Sailing from thee and home.

Over the seas to-night, love,
Dreaming beneath the spars—
Till in my dreams you shine, love,
Bright as the listening stars.

A NEGRO WOMAN'S HOSPITALITY

LEILA A. PENDLETON

Mungo Park, a native of Scotland, was one of the first of noble, brave men who devoted the best years of their lives to Africa. In 1795, when he was only twenty-four years old, he went to West Africa to find the source of the River Niger. One of the drawbacks of the west coast is its deadly climate, and shortly after arriving at Kano young Park fell ill of fever and remained an invalid for five months. While recovering, he learned the language of the Mandingoes, a native tribe, and this was a great help to him.

He finally started with only six natives on his journey. Had he been older and wiser he would have taken a larger company. At one time they were captured by Moors and a wild boar was turned loose upon them, but instead of attacking Park the beast turned upon its owners, and this aroused their superstitious fears. The king then ordered him to be put into a hut where the boar was tied while he and his chief officers discussed whether Park should lose his right hand, his eyes or his life. But he escaped from them, and after nearly two years of wandering in search of the Niger's source, during which time he suffered many hardships and had many narrow escapes, he returned to Kano, the place where he had been ill.

At one time during his journey Mr. Park arrived in the neighborhood of Sego, and as a white man had never been seen in that region before, the natives looked upon him with fear and astonishment. He asked to see the king, but no one would take him across the river, and the king sent word that he would by no means receive the strange traveler until he knew what the latter wanted.

Park was tired, hungry, and discouraged and was preparing to spend the night in the branches of a tree when a native woman pitied him. She invited him into her hut, and with the hospitality for which the natives are noted, shared with him her food. By signs she made him understand that he might occupy the sleeping mat and as she and her daughter sat spinning they sang their native songs, among them the following, which was impromptu and composed in honor of the stranger:

The wind roared and the rain fell.
The poor white man, faint and weary, came and sat under our tree.
He has no mother to bring him milk; no wife to grind his corn.

CHORUS

Let us pity the white man;
No mother has he to bring him milk;
No wife to grind his corn.

Speaking of this incident, Park says: "Trifling as this recital may appear to the reader, to a person in my situation the circumstance was affecting in the highest degree. I was oppressed by such unexpected kindness and sleep fled from my eyes." And another writer says: "The name of the woman and the alabaster box of precious ointment, the nameless widow, who, giving only two mites, had given more than all the rich, and this nameless woman of Sego, form a trio of feminine beauty and grandeur of which the sex in all ages may be proud."

RECORD OF "THE OLD FIFTEENTH" IN FRANCE

EMMETT J. SCOTT

Early in September, 1918, the men of the 369th Infantry were transferred from the 15th French Division, in which they had been serving, and made an integral part of the 161st French Division. And then, on the morning of September 26th, they joined with the Moroccans on the left and native French on the right in the offensive which won for the entire regiment the French *Croix de Guerre* and the citation of 171 individual officers and enlisted men for the *Croix de Guerre* and the Legion of Honor, for exceptional gallantry in action. The action began at Maisons-en-Champagne; it finished seven kilometers northward and eastward, and over the intervening territory the Germans had retreated before the ferocious attacks of the Fifteenth and its French comrades.

A month later a new honor came to the regiment—the honor of being the first unit of all the Allied armies to reach the River Rhine. The regiment had left its trenches at Thann, Sunday, November 17, and, marching as the advance guard of the 161st Division, Second French Army, reached the left bank of the Rhine, Monday, November 18. The 369th is proud of this achievement. It believes also that it was under fire for a greater number of days than any other American regiment. Its historian will record:

That the regiment never lost a man captured, a trench, or a foot of ground; that it was the only unit in the American Expeditionary Force which bore a State name and carried a State flag; that it was never in an American brigade or division; that it saw the first and the longest service of any American regiment as part of a foreign army; and that it had less training than any American unit before going into action.

NEGRO SOLDIERS

ROSCOE C. JAMISON

These truly are the Brave
These men who cast aside
Old memories, to walk the blood-stained pave
Of Sacrifice, joining the solemn tide
That moves away, to suffer and to die
For Freedom—when their own is yet denied!
O Pride! O Prejudice! When they pass by,
Hail them, the Brave, for you now crucified!

These truly are the Free,
These souls that grandly rise
Above base dreams of vengeance for their wrongs,
Who march to war with visions in their eyes
Of Peace through Brotherhood, lifting glad songs
Aforetime, while they front the firing-line.
Stand and behold! They take the field today,
Shedding their blood like Him now held divine,
That those who mock might find a better way!

THE "DEVIL BUSH" AND THE "GREEGREE BUSH"

GEORGE W. ELLIS

The "Devil Bush" is one of the most important social institutions of the Vais,—in fact, of most of the tribes in Liberia. It is a secret organization, and its operations are carried on in an unknown place. The penalty for divulging its secrets is said to be death. I know that it is very difficult to ascertain much information regarding it.

The aim of this society is to train young boys for African life. The boys are taught the industrial trades, native warfare, religious duties, tribal laws and customs, and the social arts.

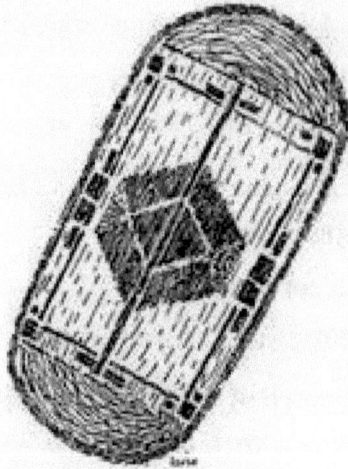

The bow and arrow may be called the Vai alphabet. Every morning the small boys are taught first to use skilfully this weapon. In addition they are taught to throw the spear and to wield the sword. In the afternoon they are taken on a hunt for small game, and later are given practice in target shooting and throwing the spear. After supper the boys take up singing and dancing. At this period they are taught also their duties to the gods, to whom a certain portion of their meals is said to be offered. Each boy is taught the sacrificial ceremony; they all clap, dance, and sing their song of praise.

When the boys have attained a certain advancement among other things they have sham battles, with 200 or 150 boys on a side. A district is given to one side to be captured by the other. Each side has a captain, and at this stage of their development emphasis is placed upon the display of bravery. And sometimes the contests assume aspects of reality. When one side repulses another six times it is said to be victorious.

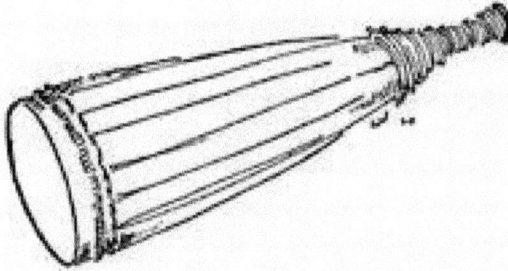

In addition to being taught the methods of warfare, the boys are taught the civil and military laws governing the Vai people. Every Vai man must know the law. And as the penalties for violating the laws covering military expeditions are so severe, the customs and laws relating thereto are of paramount importance to every Vai man.

The members of the "Devil Bush" are not only taught everything pertaining to practical war, but they are taught hunting as well. They are first taught to capture small game and later the larger and dangerous animals like the leopard, elephant, and buffalo. What the Africans call a real hunt requires about a month's work in preparation. The boys dig a large pit and surround the ends and sides with the trunks of large trees. With the pit of the apex, in triangular form, two fences are built about a mile long, and with a mile between the two extremities. The surrounding country is encircled by the hunters and the animals are driven into the pit. The smaller animals are eaten and the larger ones are sent to the king. As the valuable skins are preserved, the boys are taught to skin animals neatly. The ivories belong to the king, and various small horns are kept for amulets, and so on. These hunts are usually accompanied with much singing and dancing, after the cooking and eating of the game.

The "Greegree Bush" is a society for the training of girls for future life, just as the "Devil Bush" is for boys. It is death for a man to be found within the limits of the "Greegree Bush," no matter what his purpose may be. The sessions of the society are held near some town, yet few in that town know the exact place. No one is permitted to approach the scene.

Usually girls are admitted at seven or eight years of age, although women may be admitted.

The "Greegree Bush" has both an industrial and an educational purpose. The girls are taught to embroider with gold and silver thread the tunics and togas of kings and chiefs. Some of them become very artistic in working palm-trees, golden elephants, moons, half-moons, running vines, and other objects and scenes of nature in various articles of apparel.

The girls are taught hair-dressing in order that they may plait, beside their own, the hair of the richer Vais, some of whom have their hair oiled and plaited two or three times a week.

Instruction is given in cutting inscriptions on shields, breastplates, and the like, and in housekeeping, singing, dancing, farming, sewing, weaving cotton, dyeing, making nets and mats and many other articles of domestic utility, decoration, and dress. I have seen Vai women making some of the most beautiful fancy baskets of various kinds to be found along the coast.

EVENING PRAYER

H. CORDELIA RAY

Father of Love!
We leave our souls with Thee!
Oh! may Thy Holy Spirit to us be
A peaceful Dove!

Now when day's strife
And bitterness are o'er,
Oh! in our hearts all bruisèd gently pour
The dew of life.

So as the rose—
Though fading on the stem—
Awakes to blush when morning's lustrous gem
Upon it glows;—

May we awake,
Soothed by Thy priceless balm,
To chant with grateful hearts our morning psalm,
And blessings take.

Or let it be,
That where the palm trees rise,
And crystal streams flow, we uplift our eyes
To Thee!—to Thee!

THE STRENUOUS LIFE

SILAS X. FLOYD

They were having a rough-and-tumble time of it and Pansy was getting some pretty hard blows. She took them all good-naturedly, nevertheless, and tried to give as good as she received, much to the delight of her little boy friends. A lady who was standing near, afraid for the little girl, chided the boys and said:

"You shouldn't handle Pansy so roughly—you might hurt her."

And then Pansy looked up in sweet surprise and said with amusing seriousness:

"No; they won't hurt me. I don't break easy."

It was a thoroughly childlike expression, but it had more wisdom in it than Pansy knew. She spoke of a little girl's experience with dolls, some of which, as she had learned, broke very easily. Pansy knew how delightful it was to have a doll that didn't break so easily. Though she was not a homely girl by any means, yet she wanted it understood that she was not like a piece of china. That was why the other children liked her so much—because she knew how to rough it without crying or complaining at every turn. Pansy was not a cry-baby.

There is all the time, my dear boys and girls, a great demand everywhere all through life for people who don't break easily—people who know how to take hard knocks without going all to pieces. The game of life is sometimes rough, even among those who mean to play fair. It is very trying when we have to deal with people who break easily, and are always getting hurt and spoiling the game with their tears and complaints. It is so much better when we have to deal with people who, like little Pansy, do not break easily. Some of them will laugh off the hardest words without wincing at all. You can jostle them as you will, but they don't fall down every time you shove them, and they don't cry every time they are pushed aside. You can't but like them, they take life so heartily and so sensibly. You don't have to hold yourself in with them all the time. You can let yourself out freely without being on pins as to the result. Young people of this class make good playmates or good work-fellows, as the case may be.

So, boys and girls, you must learn to *rough* it a little. Don't be a china doll, going to smash at every hard knock. If you get hard blows take them cheerily and as easily as you can. Even if some blow comes when you least expect it, and knocks you off your feet for a minute, don't let it *floor* you long. Everybody likes the fellow who can get up when he is knocked down and blink the tears away and pitch in again. Learning to get yourself accustomed to a little hard treatment will be good for you. Hard words and hard fortune often make us—if we don't let them break us. Stand up to your work or play courageously, and when you hear words that hurt, when you are hit hard with the blunders or misdeeds of others, when life goes roughly with you, keep right on in a happy, companionable, courageous, helpful spirit, and let the world know that you don't break easily.

O LITTLE DAVID, PLAY ON YOUR HARP

JOSEPH S. COTTER, JR.

O Little David, play on your harp,
That ivory harp with the golden strings;
And sing as you did in Jewry land,
Of the Prince of Peace and the God of Love
And the Coming Christ Immanuel.
O Little David, play on your harp.

O Little David, play on your harp,
That ivory harp with the golden strings;
And psalm anew your songs of Peace,
Of the soothing calm of a Brotherly Love,
And the saving grace of a Mighty God.
O Little David, play on your harp.

A DAY AT KALK BAY, SOUTH AFRICA

L. J. COPPIN

Summer in Cape Town begins with November and lasts until March. This may seem strange to those living in North America, but a moment's reflection will suffice to remind them that during these months the sun is south of the equator, hence this natural result. The strong southeast winds, which are prevalent during the summer months, often make it very unpleasant in Cape Town on account of the dust, and one finds it most desirable occasionally to run out to one of the suburbs where "Cape Doctor" does not make such frequent and violent visits.

Of the chain of beautiful and pleasant suburban towns following the railway north, the most important as a summer resort, is Kalk Bay. One who has visited the beach at Newport, R. I., in the United States, will, upon visiting Kalk Bay, see a resemblance. Unlike the long sweep of ocean at Atlantic City, the beach is narrow, being rather a bay than an open ocean front. Instead of the cliffs as at Newport, we have the massive mountains standing almost perpendicularly on the east side, at the foot of which the town is situated.

The principal vocation among the laboring men there is fishing. In this respect it is very much like Bermuda. They go to sea and return according to the tide. Some days they are out by two and three o'clock in the morning. When they go this early they may be expected to return by noon or even before noon.

I was told that of the sixty-five fishing boats on the Bay fifty-six are owned by colored men. There are six men to a crew, five beside the captain, who is the owner of the boat. They sail out to sea, drop anchor, and fish with hook and line. Half of what is caught belongs to the captain, and the other half is equally divided among the other five men. They can scarcely supply the market, so great is the demand for fish at the Bay and in Cape Town. We were informed that a captain has been known to make as much as eight pounds in a single day; that is nearly forty dollars. Of course, there are days when they have poorer luck. Some days the wind blows such a gale that they are unable to go to sea at all.

It is a beautiful sight to see the little fleet return. Hundreds of people will gather about the landing and await their coming.

Farther up the bay, a drag net is used. On the day of our visit we were fortunate in being just in time to see a net land "full of great fishes." As the net is hauled near the shore, the fishermen all get around it, holding the lower portion of it down to keep the fish from escaping under it and holding the upper portion above the water to keep them from jumping over it. As the fish are drawn into shallow water they become very active, and notwithstanding the vigilance of the crew, some will make their escape. The captain would shout impulsively to the men; I could not understand him as he expressed himself in "Cape Dutch," but from the contortions of his face and the frightened look of the men, I guess he must have been using language that would not have been suitable in a church service. "A good haul," some one remarked when the net was finally landed.

BISHOP ATTICUS G. HAYGOOD

W. H. CROGMAN

It is indeed the peculiar glory of the truly great man, that he cannot be restricted within the State lines or race lines. Wide as the sweep of his sympathies is the empire of hearts over which he rules. To those of us, therefore, whose good fortune it was to be personally acquainted with Bishop Haygood, it was never a surprise that his influence in both sections of country and among all classes of people was so large and so commanding. He was a man of large sympathy, that royal quality in the human breast which invariably distinguishes the generous person from the mean, that divine quality which, despite our prejudices and antipathies, "makes the whole world kin," and is at the bottom of all Christian and philanthropic endeavor.

A thousand instances of kindness on the part of the good bishop to persons of all sorts and colors might, I suppose, be cited here in support of the statement made with reference to his sympathetic disposition. Many of these little acts of pure benevolence, never intended for the light, are fast coming to light under the shadow cast by his death. For as dark nights best reveal the stars, so the gloom that at times envelopes a human life discovers to us its hidden virtues.

This much, however, the world knows in common of Bishop Haygood: He was not a man who passed through life inquiring, "Who is my neighbor?" His neighbor was the ignorant that needed to be instructed, the vicious that needed to be reclaimed, the despondent that needed to be encouraged. Wherever honest effort was being made for a noble purpose, there he found his neighbor, and his neighbor found a helper. Like "The Man of Galilee," he was abroad in the land, studying the needs of the people and striving to reach and influence individual lives.

HOW TWO COLORED CAPTAINS FELL

RALPH W. TYLER

A colored unit was ordered to charge, and take, if possible, a very difficult objective held by the Germans. Captains Fairfax and Green, two colored officers, were in command of the detachments. They made the charge, running into several miles of barb-wire entanglements, and hampered by a murderous fire from nests of German machine guns which were camouflaged.

Just before charging, one of the colored sergeants, running up to Captain Fairfax, said: "Do you know there is a nest of German machine guns ahead?"

The Captain replied: "I only know we have been ordered to go forward, and we are going."

Those were the last words he said, before giving the command to charge, "into the jaws of death." The colored troops followed their intrepid leader with all the enthusiasm and dash characteristic of patriots and courageous fighters. They went forward, they obeyed the order, and as a result sixty-two men and two officers were listed in the casualties reported.

Captain Fairfax's last words, "I only know we have been ordered to go forward, and we are going," are words that will forever live in the memory of his race; they are words that match those of Sergeant Carney, the color sergeant of the 54th Massachusetts during the Civil War, who, although badly wounded, held the tattered, shot-pierced Stars and Stripes aloft and exclaimed, "The old flag never touched the ground!"

Men who have served under Captains Fairfax and Green say two braver officers never fought and fell.

THE YOUNG WARRIOR

JAMES WELDON JOHNSON

Mother, shed no mournful tears,
But gird me on my sword;
And give no utterance to thy fears,
But bless me with thy word.

The lines are drawn! The fight is on!
A cause is to be won!
Mother, look not so white and wan;
Give Godspeed to thy son.

Now let thine eyes my way pursue
Where'er my footsteps fare;
And when they lead beyond thy view,
Send after me a prayer.

But pray not to defend from harm,
Nor danger to dispel;
Pray, rather that with steadfast arm
I fight the battle well.

Pray, mother of mine, that I always keep
My heart and purpose strong,
My sword unsullied and ready to leap
Unsheathed against the wrong.

WHOLE REGIMENTS DECORATED

EMMETT J. SCOTT

Four Negro regiments won the signal honor of being awarded the *Croix de Guerre* as a regiment. These were the 365th, the 369th, the 371st and the 372d. The 369th (old 15th New York National Guard) was especially honored for its record of 191 days on the firing line, exceeding by five days the term of service at the front of any other American regiment.

ON PLANTING ARTICHOKES

FROM THE LIFE OF SCOTT BOND

DANIEL A. RUDD AND THEODORE BOND

I was living at one time on a farm, which I had bought near Forrest City, known as the Neely farm. It was also known as a fine fruit farm. The land being upland was of a poor nature. I bought the farm mainly on account of the health of my wife and children. I paid old man Neely $900 for 120 acres. This farm was two and a half miles from my main bottom farm. After moving on the Neely place and getting straight, I looked over the farm and finding that the land was far from fertile, I decided to sow the whole farm in peas, knowing peas were a legume and hence fine to put life into the soil. I excepted several small spots that I planted in corn.

I got a fine stand of peas, and looked as if I would make worlds of pea hay. When the peas were ripe I took my mower and rake to harvest my hay crop. This was the first time I had undertaken to cultivate this class of land. I prepared to house the hay and after the hay was cut and raked, I only got one-tenth of the amount of hay I counted on. I prepared the land that fall and sowed it down in clover. I got a fine stand. The clover grew and did well. The next year I took two four-horse wagons and hauled from the Allen farm large loads of defective cotton seed. I turned all this under and planted the land the next year in corn. I made and gathered a large corn crop that year.

I was at that time taking a farm paper and I would usually sit at night and entertain my wife, while she was sewing. I read an article, where a party in Illinois had claimed that he had gathered 900 bushels of artichokes from one acre of land. That did not look reasonable to me at that time. I said to my wife: "Listen to what a mistake this fellow has made. He claims to have gathered 900 bushels of artichokes from one acre of land." This seemed impossible to me.

In the next issue of this paper I read where another man claimed to have raised 1,100 bushels to the acre. This put me at a further wonder as to the artichoke crop. I decided to try a crop of artichokes. I had a very nice spot of land that I thought would suit me for this purpose. I prepared it as I would prepare land for Irish potatoes, knowing that artichokes were, like the Irish potato, a tuber. I took a four-horse wagon and hauled one and a half tons of rotten cotton seed, and of this I put a double handful every 18 inches apart in the drill; I then dropped the artichokes between the hills. I cultivated first as I would Irish potatoes. The plants grew luxuriantly and were all the way from 8 to 12 feet tall.

About the 10th of August I noticed the plants were blooming and it occurred to me that there must be artichokes on the roots. I got my spade and began to dig. I could not find a single artichoke. I took my spade back home and decided within myself that both parties were mistaken when they claimed to have grown so many hundreds of bushels to the acre. After a few days I went to my lower farm and started picking cotton, and was as busy as busy could be all that fall gathering and housing my cotton crop as usual.

Just before Christmas I promised my wife that I would be at home on Christmas Eve in order to accompany her to our church conference. I was on time according to my promise, helped her to get her household affairs straight and the children settled. I had bought my wife a beautiful cape. She took the cape, I took my overcoat and off we went. In order to take a near route we decided to climb the fence and go through the artichoke patch. As we had none of the children along I, helping her over the fence, recalled our old days when we were courting. I remarked to her:

"Gee whiz, wife, you certainly look good under that cape!"

She said, "Do you think so?"

"Yes, I have always thought that you looked good."

By this time we had gotten to the middle of the artichoke patch. I grabbed an artichoke stalk and tried to pull it up. I made one or two surges and it failed to come, but in bending it over I found a great number of artichokes attached to the tap root. I asked my wife to wait a few minutes. She asked me what I was going to do. I told her I would run back and get the grubbing hoe and see what is under these artichokes. She said, "Doesn't this beat the band? Stop on your way to church to go to digging artichokes."

"All right, I will be back in a few minutes."

I came with my grubbing hoe and went to work. I dug on all sides of the stalk, then raised it up. I believe I am safe in saying there was a half bushel of artichokes on the roots of this stalk. I then noticed that the dirt in the drills, the sides of the rows, and the middles were all puffed up. One could not stick the end of his finger in the ground without touching an artichoke. I found that the whole earth was matted with artichokes. I really believe that had I had a full acre in and could have gathered all the artichokes, I would have gotten at least 1,500 bushels.

I told my wife that now I could see that those people had told the truth when they said they had gathered 900 bushels and 1,100 bushels to the acre.

When I returned from church, I at once turned my hogs into the artichoke patch. I then climbed up on the fence and took a seat to watch the hogs root and crush artichokes. I looked around and saw my clover had made a success, the little artichoke patch had turned out wonderfully. I said to myself: "Just think of millions and millions of dollars deposited in all these lands, both rich and poor soils. And just to think how easy this money could be obtained if one would think right and hustle."

A SONG OF THANKS

EDWARD SMYTH JONES

For the sun that shone at the dawn of spring,
For the flowers which bloom and the birds that sing,
For the verdant robe of the grey old earth,
For her coffers filled with their countless worth,
For the flocks which feed on a thousand hills,
For the rippling streams which turn the mills,
For the lowing herds in the lovely vale,
For the songs of gladness on the gale,—
From the Gulf and the Lakes to the Oceans' banks,—
Lord God of Hosts, we give Thee thanks!

For the farmer reaping his whitened fields,
For the bounty which the rich soil yields,
For the cooling dews and refreshing rains,
For the sun which ripens the golden grains,
For the bearded wheat and the fattened swine,
For the stallèd ox and the fruitful vine,
For the tubers large and cotton white,
For the kid and the lambkin, frisk and blithe,
For the swan which floats near the river-banks,—
Lord God of Hosts, we give Thee thanks!

For the pumpkin sweet and the yellow yam,
For the corn and beans and the sugared ham,
For the plum and the peach and the apple red,
For the clustering nut trees overhead.
For the cock which crows at the breaking dawn,
And the proud old "turk" of the farmer's barn,
For the fish which swim in the babbling brooks,
For the game which hides in the shady nooks,—
From the Gulf and the Lakes to the Oceans' banks,—
Lord God of Hosts, we give Thee thanks!

For the sturdy oaks and the stately pines,
For the lead and the coal from the deep, dark mines,
For the silver ores of a thousand fold,
For the diamond bright and the yellow gold,
For the river boat and the flying train,
For the fleecy sail of the rolling main,

For the velvet sponge and the glossy pearl,
For the flag of peace which we now unfurl,—
From the Gulf and the Lakes to the Oceans' Banks,—
Lord God of Hosts, we give Thee thanks!

For the lowly cot and the mansion fair,
For the peace and plenty together share,
For the Hand which guides us from above,
For Thy tender mercies, abiding love,
For the blessed home with its children gay,
For returnings of Thanksgiving Day,
For the bearing toils and the sharing cares,
We lift up our hearts in our songs and our prayers,—
From the Gulf and the Lakes to the Oceans' banks,—
Lord God of Hosts, we give Thee thanks!

OUR DUMB ANIMALS

SILAS X. FLOYD

Domestic animals—like horses, cats and dogs—seem to be almost as dependent upon kind treatment and affection as human beings. Horses and dogs especially are the most keenly intelligent of our dumb friends, and are alike sensitive to cruelty in any form. They are influenced to an equal degree by kind and affectionate treatment.

If there is any form of cruelty that is more blameworthy than another, it is abuse of a faithful horse who gives his life to the service of the owner. When a horse is pulling a heavy load with all his might, doing the best he can to move under it, to strike him, spur him, or swear at him is barbarous. To kick a dog around or strike him with sticks just for the fun of hearing him yelp or seeing him run, is equally barbarous. No high-minded man, no high-minded boy or girl, would do such a thing.

We should never forget how helpless, in a large sense, dumb animals are— and how absolutely dependent upon the humanity and kindness of their owners. They are really the slaves of man, having no language by which to express their feelings or needs.

The poet Cowper said:

"I would not enter on my list of friends,
Though graced with polished manners and fine sense,
Yet wanting sensibility, the man
Who needlessly sets foot upon a worm."

Boys and girls should be willing to pledge themselves to be kind to all harmless living creatures, and every boy and girl should strive to protect such creatures from cruel usage on the part of others. It is noble, boys and girls, for us to speak for those that cannot speak for themselves, and it is noble, also, for us to protect those that cannot protect themselves.

A LEGEND OF THE BLUE JAY

RUTH ANNA FISHER

It was a hot, sultry day in May and the children in the little school in Virginia were wearily waiting for the gong to free them from lessons for the day. Furtive glances were directed towards the clock. The call of the birds and fields was becoming more and more insistent. Would the hour never strike!

"The Planting of the Apple-tree" had no interest for them. Little attention was given the boy as he read in a sing-song, spiritless manner:

"What plant we in this apple-tree?
Buds, which the breath of summer days
Shall lengthen into leafy sprays;
Boughs where the thrush, with crimson breast,
Shall haunt and sing and hide her nest."

The teacher, who had long since stopped trying to make the lesson interesting, found herself saying mechanically, "What other birds have their nests in the apple-tree?"

The boy shifted lazily from one foot to the other as he began, "The sparrow, the robin, and wrens, and—the snow-birds and blue-jays—"

"No, they don't, blue-jays don't have nests," came the excited outburst from some of the children, much to the surprise of the teacher.

When order was restored some of these brown-skinned children, who came from the heart of the Virginian mountains, told this legend of the blue-jay.

Long, long years ago, the devil came to buy the blue-jay's soul, for which he first offered a beautiful golden ear of corn. This the blue-jay liked and wanted badly, but said, "No, I cannot take it in exchange for my soul." Then the devil came again, this time with a bright red ear of corn which was even more lovely than the golden one.

This, too, the blue-jay refused. At last the devil came to offer him a wonderful blue ear. This one the blue-jay liked best of all, but still was unwilling to part with his soul. Then the devil hung it up in the nest, and the blue-jay found that it exactly matched his own brilliant feathers, and knew at once that he must have it. The bargain was quickly made. And now in payment for that one blue ear of corn each Friday the blue-jay must carry one grain of sand to the devil, and sometimes he gets back on Sunday, but oftener not until Monday.

Very seriously the children added, "And all the bad people are going to burn until the blue-jays have carried all the grains of sand in the ocean to the devil."

The teacher must have smiled a little at the legend, for the children cried out again, "It is so. 'Deed it is, for doesn't the black spot on the blue-jay come because he gets his wings scorched, and he doesn't have a nest like other birds."

Then, to dispel any further doubts the teacher might have, they asked triumphantly, "You never saw a blue-jay on Friday, did you?"

There was no need to answer, for just then the gong sounded and the children trooped happily out to play.

DAVID LIVINGSTONE

BENJAMIN BRAWLEY

When Livingstone began his work of exploration in 1849, practically all of Africa between the Sahara and the Dutch settlements in the extreme South was unknown territory. By the time of his death in 1873 he had brought this entire region within the view of civilization. On his first journey, or series of journeys (1849-1856,) starting from Cape Town, he made his way northward for a thousand miles to Lake Ngami; then pushing on to Linyanti, he undertook one of the most perilous excursions of his entire career, his objective for more than a thousand miles being Loanda on the West Coast, which point he reached after six months in the wilderness.

Coming back to Linyanti, he turned his face eastward, discovered Victoria Falls on the Zambesi, and finally arrived at Cuilimane on the coast. On his second series of journeys (1858-1864) he explored the Zambesi, the Shire, and the Rovuma rivers in the East, and discovered Lake Nyasa. On his final expedition (1866-1873), in hunting for the upper courses of the Nile, he discovered Lakes Tanganyika, Mweru, and Bangweolo, and the Lualaba River. His achievement as an explorer was as distinct as it was unparalleled. His work as a missionary and his worth as a man it is not quite so easy to express concretely; but in these capacities he was no less distinguished and his accomplishment no less signal.

There had been missionaries, and great ones, in Africa before Livingstone. The difference between Livingstone and consecrated men was not so much in devotion as in the conception of the task. He himself felt that a missionary in the Africa of his day was to be more than a mere preacher of the word— that he would have also to be a Christian statesman, and even a director of exploration and commerce if need be. This was his title to greatness; to him "the end of the geographical feat was only the beginning of the enterprise." Knowing, however, that many honest persons did not sympathize with him in this conception of his mission, after 1856 he declined longer to accept salary from the missionary society that originally sent him out, working afterwards under the patronage of the British Government and the Royal Geographical Society.

His sympathy and his courtesy were unfailing, even when he himself was placed in the greatest danger. Said Henry Drummond of him: "Wherever David Livingstone's footsteps are crossed in Africa the fragrance of his memory seems to remain." On one occasion a hunter was impaled on the horn of a rhinoceros, and a messenger ran eight miles for the physician. Although he himself had been wounded for life by a lion and his friends insisted that he should not ride at night through a wood infested with wild beasts, Livingstone insisted on his Christian duty to go, only to find that the man had died and to have to retrace his footsteps.

Again and again his party would have been destroyed by some savage chieftain if it had not been for his own unbounded tact and courage. To the devoted men who helped him he gave the assurance that he would die before he would permit them to be taken; and after his death at Chitambo's village Susi and Chuma journeyed for nine months and over eight hundred miles of dangerous country to take his body to the coast.

Livingstone was a man of tremendous faith, in his mission, in his country, in humanity, in God. He wrote on one occasion: "This age presents one great fact in the Providence of God; missions are sent forth to all quarters of the world,—missions not of one section of the Church, but from all sections, and from nearly all Christian nations. It seems very unfair to judge of the success of these by the number of the conversions that have followed. These are rather proofs of the missions being of the right sort. The fact which ought to stimulate us above all others is, not that we have contributed to the conversion of a few souls, however valuable these may be, but that we are diffusing a knowledge of Christianity throughout the world. Future missionaries will see conversions follow every sermon. We prepare the way for them. We work for a glorious future which we are not destined to see— the golden age which has not been, but will yet be. We are only morning-stars shining in the dark, but the glorious morn will break, the good time coming yet. For this time we work; may God accept our imperfect service."

Of such quality was David Livingstone—Missionary, Explorer, Philanthropist. "For thirty years his life was spent in an unwearied effort to evangelize the native races, to explore the undiscovered secrets, and abolish the desolating slave trade of Central Africa." To what extent after sixty years have we advanced toward his ideals? With what justice are we the inheritors of his renown?

IRA ALDRIDGE

WILLIAM J. SIMMONS

The name of Aldridge has always been placed at the head of the list of Negro actors. He has indeed become the most noted of them, and his name is cited as standing first in his calling among all colored persons who have ever appeared on the stage. He was born at Belaire, near Baltimore, in 1804. In complexion he was dark brown, and with heavy whiskers; standing six feet in height, with heavy frame, African features, and yet with due proportions; he was graceful in his attitudes, highly polished in manners.

In his early days he was apprenticed to a ship carpenter, and had his association with the Germans on the western shores of Maryland. Here he became familiar with the German language and spoke it not only with ease but with fluency. He was brought in contact with Edmund Kean, the great actor, in 1826, whom he accompanied in his trip through Europe. His ambition to become an actor was encouraged by Kean, and receiving his assistance in the preparation, he made his appearance first at the Royalty Theatre in London, in the character of Othello. Public applause greeted him of such an extraordinary nature, that he was billed to appear at the Covent Garden Theatre April 10, 1839, in the same character.

After many years' successful appearances in many of the metropolitan cities, he appeared in the Provinces with still greater success. In Ireland he performed Othello, with Edmund Kean as Iago. In 1852 he appeared in Germany in Shakespearean characters. He was pronounced excellent, and though a stranger and a foreigner, he undertook the very difficult task of playing in English, while his whole support was rendered in the language of the country. It is said that until this time, such an experiment was not considered susceptible of a successful end, but nevertheless, with his impersonations he succeeded admirably. It is said that the King of Prussia was so deeply moved with his appearance in the character of Othello, at Berlin, that he spent him a congratulatory letter, and conferred upon him the title of chevalier, in recognition of his dramatic genius, and informed him that the lady who took the part of Desdemona was so much affected at the manner in which he played his part that she was made ill from fright on account of the reality with which he acted his part.

Some idea of the character of his acting might be gained from the fact that the lady who played Desdemona in St. Petersburg, became very much alarmed at what appeared real passion on his part, in acting Othello; though he was never rough or indelicate in any of his acting with ladies, yet she was so frightened that she used to scream with real fear.

It is said that on another occasion in St. Petersburg, that in the midst of his acting in scene two, act five, when he was quoting these words,

"It is the cause, it is the cause, my soul;
Let me not name it to you, you chaste stars!
It is the cause. Yet I'll not shed her blood,
Nor scar that whiter skin of hers than snow,
And smooth as monumental alabaster.
Yet she must die, else she'll betray more men.
Put out the light, and then—put out the light!
If I quench thee, thou flaming minister,
I can again thy former light restore,
Should I repent me: But once put out thy light,
Thou cunning'st pattern of excelling nature;
I know not where is that Promethean heat,
That can thy light relume. When I have plucked thy rose,
I cannot give it vital growth again;
It needs must wither:—
I'll smell it on the tree—
(*kissing her*)
O balmy breath, that dost almost persuade
Justice to break her sword:—
One more, one more:—
Be thus when thou art dead, and I will kill thee,
And love thee after:—
One more—and this the last:
So sweet was ne'er so fatal. I must weep.
But they are cruel tears:
This sorrow's heavenly:
It strikes where it doth love."

the house was so carried away with the manner in which he rendered it, that a young man stood up and exclaimed with the greatest earnestness: "She is innocent, Othello, she is innocent," and yet so interested was he in the acting himself that he never moved a muscle but continued as if nothing had been said to embarrass him. The next day he learned, while dining with a Russian prince, that a young man who had been present had been so affected by the play that he had been seized with a sudden illness and died the next day.

Mr. Aldridge was a welcome guest in the ranks of the cultured and wealthy, and was often in the "salons" of the haughty aristocrats of St. Petersburg and Moscow. Titled ladies wove, knitted and stitched their pleasing emotions into various memorials of friendship. In his palatial residence at Sydenham, near London, were collected many presents of intrinsic value, rendered almost sacred by association. Prominent among these tokens of regard was an autographic letter from the King of Prussia, transmitting the first medal of art and sciences; the Cross of Leopold, from the Emperor of Russia, and a Maltese cross received at Berne.

In all his triumphs he never lost interest in the condition of his race. He always took an interest in everything touching their welfare, and though exalted to the companionship of those who ranked high in every department of life, yet he never in any way forgot the humble race with which he was identified, and was always solicitous for their welfare and promotion. He was an associate of the most prominent men of Paris, among whom was Alexander Dumas. When the great tragedian and great writer met they always kissed each other, and Dumas always greeted Aldridge with the words Mon Confrère. He died at Lodes, in Poland, August 7, 1867.

FIFTY YEARS

1863-1913

JAMES WELDON JOHNSON

O brothers mine, to-day we stand
Where half a century sweeps our ken,
Since God, through Lincoln's ready hand,
Struck off our bonds and made us men.

Just fifty years—a winter's day—
As runs the history of a race;
Yet, as we look back o'er the way,
How distant seems our starting place!

Look farther back! Three centuries!
To where a naked, shivering score,
Snatched from their haunts across the seas,
Stood wild-eyed, on Virginia's shore.

Far, far the way that we have trod,
From heathen kraals and jungle dens,
To freedmen, freemen, sons of God,
Americans and Citizens.

A part of His unknown design,
We've lived within a mighty age;
And we have helped to write a line
On history's most wondrous page.

A few black bondmen strewn along
The borders of our eastern coast,
Now grown a race, ten million strong,
An upward, onward marching host.

Then let us here erect a stone,
To mark the place, to mark the time;
A witness to God's mercies shown,
A pledge to hold this day sublime.

And let that stone an altar be,
Whereon thanksgivings we may lay,

Where we, in deep humility,
For faith and strength renewed may pray.

With open hearts ask from above
New zeal, new courage and new pow'rs,
That we may grow more worthy of
This country and this land of ours.

For never let the thought arise
That we are here on sufferance bare;
Outcasts, asylumed 'neath these skies
And aliens without part or share.

This land is ours by right of birth,
This land is ours by right of toil;
We helped to turn its virgin earth,
Our sweat is in its fruitful soil.

Where once the tangled forest stood,—
Where flourished once rank weed and thorn,—
Behold the path-traced, peaceful wood,
The cotton white, the yellow corn.

To gain these fruits that have been earned,
To hold these fields that have been won,
Our arms have strained, our backs have burned,
Bent bare beneath a ruthless sun.

That Banner which is now the type
Of victory on field and flood—
Remember, its first crimson stripe
Was dyed by Attucks' willing blood.

And never yet has come the cry—
When that fair flag has been assailed—
For men to do, for men to die,
That have we faltered or have failed.

We've helped to bear it, rent and torn,
Through many a hot-breath'd battle breeze;
Held in our hands, it has been borne
And planted far across the seas.

And never yet—O haughty Land,
Let us, at least, for this be praised—
Has one black, treason-guided hand
Ever against that flag been raised.

Then should we speak but servile words,
Or shall we hang our heads in shame?
Stand back of new-come foreign hordes,
And fear our heritage to claim?

No! stand erect and without fear,
And for our foes let this suffice—
We've bought a rightful sonship here,
And we have more than paid the price.

And yet, my brothers, well I know
The tethered feet, the pinioned wings,
The spirit bowed beneath the blow,
The heart grown faint from wounds and stings;

The staggering force of brutish might,
That strikes and leaves us stunned and dazed;
The long, vain waiting through the night
To hear some voice for justice raised.

Full well I know the hour when hope
Sinks dead, and 'round us everywhere
Hangs stifling darkness, and we grope
With hands uplifted in despair.

Courage! Look out, beyond, and see
The far horizon's beckoning span!
Faith in your God-known destiny!
We are a part of some great plan.

Because the tongues of Garrison
And Phillips now are cold in death,
Think you their work can be undone?
Or quenched the fires lit by their breath?

Think you that John Brown's spirit stops?
That Lovejoy was but idly slain?

Or do you think those precious drops
From Lincoln's heart were shed in vain?

That for which millions prayed and sighed,
That for which tens of thousands fought,
For which so many freely died,
God cannot let it come to naught.

A GREAT KINGDOM IN THE CONGO

WILLIAM HENRY SHEPPARD

I had studied the new dialect of the Bakuba and had made every preparation for our expedition into the "Forbidden Land" of King Lukenga. I had met their people, a far interior tribe, and was interested in their apparent superiority in physique, manners, dress and dialect. I asked to be allowed to accompany them to their country and king, but they said it was impossible, their king would never allow a foreigner to come into the interior. Nevertheless I determined to seek them out and after some weeks had elapsed, I called our station natives together and laid plainly before them the perils of the journey. I told them, from the information which I had, that the trails which had been made by elephant, buffalo, antelope and Bakuba natives were many and they led over long, hot, sandy plains through deep dark forests, across streams without bridges, and through swamps infested with wild animals and poisonous serpents. And above all, the king had sent word throughout the land that we could not enter his country. Not a man's muscle moved, and there was not a dissenting voice.

I had picked up the Bakuba dialect from some of the king's traders and tax collectors who journeyed our way. I received from them much information of the general direction leading north toward the capital, the names of large towns on the way, of the market towns, the approximate distances apart, the streams to be crossed, and their names; of the leopard, buffalo and elephant zones, and the names of some of the chiefs of the market towns, etc.

Two days later, when all was in readiness, tents loaded, cooking utensils, a bag of money (cowrie shells), some salt, etc., we left Luebo, led by the Master's hand.

The trail lay northeast by north with a gradual ascent. The country was well wooded and watered. No stones could be seen anywhere, and the soil was sandy. There were many extensive plains with magnificent palm trees, hundreds and thousands of them ranging from a foot high, which the elephants fed upon, to those fifty and sixty feet high. The forest everywhere was ever green. Trees blossomed and bloomed, sending out upon the gentle breeze their fragrance, so acceptable to the traveler. Festoons of moss and running vines made the forest look like a beautifully painted theatre or an enormous swinging garden.

In the meantime word had come to the king of Lukenga of our presence and, as we neared his kingdom, we were met by a party of fighting men. My caravan had been resting in the village of a chief named Kueta, who had repeatedly urged me to turn back, and, as the righting men of King Lukenga appeared, the chief's men fled to the forest. I sat quietly, however, in my seat in front of my tent and my people began to gather around my chair, the youngest of the caravan nestling on his knees very close to me. The king's people drew near and the leading man, spear in hand, called to Chief Kueta in a voice that rang through the village:

"Now hear the words of King Lukenga: Because you have entertained a foreigner in your village, we have come to take you to the capital for trial."

I knew things were now serious, so rising from my seat I called to the head man to meet me half way. He paid no attention. I called a second time and walked up to him and began to plead for Chief Kueta.

"I understand you are sent by your king to arrest these people."

"It is the word of the king," said he.

I continued, "The chief of this village is not guilty; he gave me warning and told me to go away, to return the way I had come, and I did not. It is my fault and not Kueta's."

The leader, leaning on his spear, replied,

"You speak our language?"

"I do," was my quick answer.

"That is strange," said he.

The leader and his men moved off some distance and talked between themselves. In a little while he came back to me saying, "I will return to the capital and report these things to the king."

I said to him, "Tell your king I am not a bad man; I do not steal or kill; I have a message for him. Wait a moment," said I. Taking from one of my boxes a very large cowrie shell, near the size of one's fist, and holding it up, I said, "This we call the father of cowries; present it to the king as a token of friendship."

The men were soon off for the capital and we settled down, hoping and praying for the best. Kueta told me that the head man was King Lukenga's son and his name was N'Toinzide.

N'Toinzide stood more than six feet, of bronze color, blind in one eye, determined set lips, and seemed a man fearless of any foe—man or beast. The villagers told me many things of the king's son, both good and bad.

After some days the messengers reached the capital and reported to King Lukenga. "We saw the foreigner; he speaks our language, he knows all the trails of the country."

The king was astonished and called a council and laid the matter before them. They deliberated over the affair and finally told the king that they knew who I was.

"The foreigner who is at Bixibing," said they, "who has come these long trails and who speaks our language is a Makuba, one of the early settlers who died, and whose spirit went to a foreign country and now he has returned."

The messengers hastened to return and accompany me to the capital.

We had been longing and praying for days for the best. With the king's special envoy were many more men who had come through mere curiosity, as was their custom.

N'Toinzide stood in the center of the town and called with his loud voice saying who I was and giving briefly my history.

The villagers were indeed happy. They flocked around as the king's son drew near and extended their hands to me.

I arose from my chair and made these remarks: "I have heard distinctly all that you have said, but I am not a Makuba; I have never been here before."

N'Toinzide insisted that they were right, and said that his father, the king, wanted me to come on at once to the capital. The people were mighty happy, Kueta, our host, the townspeople, and my people, too. Their appetites came back, and so did mine.

With a hasty good-bye, "Gala hola," to Kueta, we were off.

On the last morning our trail grew larger, the country more open, and the ascent greater, until we stood upon an extensive plain and had a beautiful view in every direction of all the land as far as we could see.

We could see in the distance thousands and thousands of banana and palm trees and our escort of Bakuba cried out, "Muxenge! muxenge!" (meaning capital! capital!). Just before entering the great town we were halted at a small guard post consisting of a few houses and some men who were the king's watchmen. They told me that on each of the four entrances to the capital these sentries were stationed. A man was dispatched to notify the king that we were near. In a short while the people came out of the town to meet and greet us, hundreds of them, and many little children, too. Some of my caravan were frightened and would run away, but I told them that the oncoming crowd meant no harm.

N'Toinzide, the king's son, with spear in hand, took the lead and the interested and excited crowd after getting a peep at me fell in behind.

We marched down a broad, clean street, lined on both sides by interested spectators jostling, gesticulating, talking aloud and laughing. The young boys and girls struck up a song which sounded to me like a band of sweet music and we all kept step to it. N'Toinzide called a halt at a house which I presume was 15 x 25 feet in size. You could enter the doors front and back almost without stooping. The house was made like all the others of bamboo and had two rooms. There were a number of clay pots of various sizes for cooking and six large gourds for water. My caravan was comfortably housed. I did not put up my tent, but took my seat in a reclining chair under a large palm tree in front of my door. The crowd was immense, but we had them sit down on the ground so we could get a breath of air.

In the afternoon the king sent greetings, and fourteen goats, six sheep, a number of chickens, corn, pumpkins, large dried fish, bushels of peanuts, bunches of bananas and plantains and a calabash of palm oil and other food.

The prime minister, N'Dola, who brought the greetings, mentioned that the king would see me next day; also that the king's servants would take out of the village all goats and chickens which I did not want for immediate use.

For, said N'Dola, no sheep, goats, hogs, dogs, ducks or chickens are allowed in the king's town.

In the evening we started our song service and I delivered to them our King's message. The crowd was great. The order was good. I went to rest with the burden of these people upon my heart, and thanking God that He had led, protected and brought us through close places safely to the "Forbidden Land."

Early in the morning we heard the blast of ivory horns calling the attention of the people to put on their best robes and be in readiness for the big parade. I saw there was great activity in the town, men and women hurrying to and fro. Soon two stalwart Bakuba, with their red kilts on and feathers in their hats appeared before my house and announced their readiness to accompany me before King Lukenga.

They noticed an old brass button tied by a string around the neck of one of my men. Very politely they removed it, saying, "Only the king can wear brass or copper."

I was dressed in what had once been white linen. Coat, trousers, white canvas shoes and pith helmet. The officials on either side took me by the arm; we walked a block up the broad street, turned to the right and walked three blocks till we came to the big town square. Thousands of the villagers had already taken their position and were seated on the green grass. King Lukenga, his high officials and about 300 of his wives occupied the eastern section of the square. The players of stringed instruments and drummers were in the center, and as we appeared a great shout went up from the people. The king's servants ran and spread leopard skins along the ground leading to his majesty. I approached with some timidity. The king arose from his throne of ivory, stretched forth his hand and greeted me with these words, "Wyni" (You have come). I bowed low, clapped my hands in front of me, and answered, "Ndini, Nyimi" (I have come, king).

As the drums beat and the harps played the king's sons entered the square and danced one after the other single handed, brandishing their big knives in the air. The king's great chair, or throne, was made of carved tusks of ivory, and his feet rested upon lion skins. I judged him to have been a little more than six feet high and with his crown, which was made of eagle feathers, he towered over all. The king's dress consisted of a red loin cloth, draped neatly about his waist in many folds. He wore a broad belt decorated with cowrie shells and beads. His armlets and anklets were made of polished cowrie shells reaching quite above the wrists and ankles. These decorations were beautifully white. His feet were painted with powdered canwood, resembling morocco boots. The king weighed about 200 pounds. He wore a pleasant smile. He looked to be eighty years old, but he was as active as a middle-aged man.

As the sun was setting in the west the king stood up, made a slight bow to his people and to me. His slaves were ready with his cowrie-studded hammock to take him to his place, for his feet must never touch the ground. His hammock was like the body of a buggy carried on two long poles upon the shoulders of many men. Through the shouts of the people I was accompanied back to my resting place. It was the most brilliant affair I had seen in Africa, but my! I was so glad when it was all over.

The town was laid off east and west. The broad streets ran at right angles, and there were blocks just as in any town. Those in a block were always related in some way. Around each house is a court and a high fence made of heavy matting of palm leaves, and around each block there is also a high fence, so you enter these homes by the many gates. Each block has a chief called Mbambi, and he is responsible to King Lukenga for his block. When the king will deliver a message to the whole village or part of it, these chiefs are sent for and during the early evenings they ring their iron hand bells and call out in a loud voice the message in five minutes. The king desired of his own heart to give me peanuts for my people. I heard the messengers delivering the word and the next morning we had more peanuts than we could manage.

There was not a visible light anywhere in the whole town. "A chunk or two" is always kept smouldering in the center of the house on the clay floor. The housewife is always careful to have a handful of split dry bamboo near, and when anyone is stung by a scorpion or snake (which often happens) they start up a blaze and hunt for the intruder and medicine.

When there is neither moon nor stars it is truly a land of awful darkness, and is made more dismal by the yelping of the jackal on the plain. The moon shines more brightly and beautifully than on Lukenga's plain. And the beauty is enhanced by the thousands of majestic palms, and the singing of birds with voices like the mocking bird and the nightingale. I have sat in front of my house moonlight nights until 12 and 1 o'clock.

Every morning the "courts" and streets were swept. Men who had committed some offense were compelled to pull weeds and sweep the streets clean.

There is a rule in all Bakuba villages that every man every day sweep before his own door. The only littered places I observed were at the four public entrances of the town where markets were held daily at 6 A.M., 12 noon and 5 P.M.—sugar cane, pulp, banana and plantain peelings, and peanut shells.

When the king's drum taps the signal about 9 P.M. at the conclusion of the sleep song there is not a sound again in the whole village.

All the natives we have met in the Kasal are, on the whole, honest. Our private dwellings have never been locked day or night. Your pocketbook is a sack of cowries or salt tied at the mouth with a string. But now and then something happens. N'susa, one of the boys of my caravan, misappropriated some cowries. I called him (in the presence of two witnesses) in question about the matter. He acknowledged removing the shells and innocently remarked, "You are the same as my father, and what is his is mine."

From the great Lukenga plateau as far as the eye can look you see villages dotted everywhere. You never find a family living alone isolated from the village. The people live together for mutual protection from enemies and animals. And usually everybody in a village is related in some near or distant way; but it does not keep them from fighting occasionally.

The Bakuba are monogamists. A young man sees a girl whom he likes; he has met her in his own town or at some other, or perhaps at a market place or a dance. He sends her tokens of love, bananas, plantains, peanuts, dried fish or grasshoppers. She in turn sends him similar presents.

They often meet, sit down on the green, laugh and talk together. I have seen the girls often blush and really put on airs. He asks her to have him, if she has no one else on her heart, and tells her that he wants no one to eat the crop that is in the field but her. The girl and the parents both agree.

On a set day when the market is in full blast, with hundreds of people from everywhere, the young man and girl, with their young friends, all dressed in their best robes, meet and march Indian file through the open market and receive congratulations from everybody.

The new bride and groom continue their march to the already prepared house of the young man. A feast of goat, sheep, monkey, chicken or fish, with plenty of palm wine is served and all is ended with a big dance.

The women of the king's household select their own husbands, and no man dare decline; and no man would ever be so rude or presumptuous as to ask for the hand and heart of royalty.

The husband knows that he must cut down the forest and assist in planting corn, millet, beans, pease, sweet potatoes and tobacco, hunt for game, bring the palm wine, palm nuts, make his wife's garments and repair the house. He is never to be out after 8 o'clock at night unless sitting up at a wake or taking part in a public town dance.

The young man before marriage sends a certain number of well-woven mats and so many thousands of cowries to the parents of the girl as a dowry. If they cease to love and must part, even twenty rainy seasons from marriage, the dowry or its equivalent is returned to the man.

The wife is expected to shave and anoint the husband's body with palm oil, keep his toenails and fingernails manicured, bring water and wood, help in the field, cook his food, and take care of the children.

I have had many a man come and ask to buy love medicine. They think charms and medicine can do anything. I always told them, of course, that it was a matter of the girl's heart, and charms or medicine could not help out in their "love affairs."

The Bakuba are morally a splendid people. I have asked a number of Bakuba what was their real ideal of life, and they invariably answered to have a big corn field, marry a good wife, and have many children.

We were astounded when we saw the first new-born baby. It was so very light. But in a few weeks the youngster rallied to his colors and we were assured that he would never change again.

No baby is born in the regularly occupied house. A small house is built in the back yard and is surrounded by a fence of palm fronds. No one is admitted into the enclosure but a few women. The new youngster receives a bath of palm oil, then the notice is given and all the friends of the family with jugs of cold water vie with each other in giving mother and baby a shower bath. The drums beat and the dance in water and mud continues for hours.

Until you get accustomed to it you would be horrified to see the mothers stuff their young babies. The mother nurses the baby just as any mother, but she doesn't think that sufficient. So she has by her side a small pot of soft corn pone and a pot of water or palm oil. She makes a large pill from the pone, dips it in the water or oil, and while the baby is lying on his back in her lap these pills are dropped in its mouth. Then the mother uses the forefinger to force the collection of pills down its throat. As the baby resists and kicks, water is poured down its throat to facilitate the process. If the baby strangles, the mother will shake him up and down a few times. When the feeding is over, he certainly looks "stuffed."

The Bakuba children have many games and but few toys. The girls have wooden dolls made by their fathers, and the boys make from bamboo bows and arrows. They shoot mice, lizards, grasshoppers, crickets, caterpillars, butterflies, lightning bugs, etc.

They make mud pies and play market, and tie the legs of May and June bugs to see them fly around and buzz. They love to play housekeeping. They are also trained to do some work, as bringing wood, sweeping or looking after the younger ones. There are no knives, forks or dishes to wash.

"Baby talk" is not used and the parents speak to the babies just as though they were speaking to grown-ups.

I have seen the children in the streets drawing with a pointed stick or their finger on the smooth sand, men, leopards, monkeys, crocodiles, birds, snakes and other animals.

The boys make a heap of clay and sod it, and with great speed run upon it and turn a somersault, lighting on their feet. A string of them together will play "leap frog," and hide-and-seek is great sport with them. In all these amusements they keep up a song.

There is one thing you will certainly see them doing, both boys and girls, and that is beating their clenched fists into the hard clay just as hard as they can drive. A year later you will see them driving their knuckles against a log or a tree. In this way they become hardened and are used as a weapon in fights when they are grown. And, too, they can butt like a goat, so in their family fights they not only use their fists but their heads.

I spent hours at King Lukenga's and other villages playing with the little folks and trying to find out what they were thinking about. They had a name for the sun and moon, names for very brilliant and prominent stars and ordinary ones. The sun was the father of the heavens, the moon was his wife, and the stars were their children. The sun after going down was paddled around in a very large canoe on the great water by men who were more than human and started in the skies again. They knew that a year was divided into two general seasons, the rainy (eight moons), the dry (four moons); though even in the rainy season it doesn't rain every day and very seldom all day at any time; and in the dry season there is an occasional refreshing shower.

They knew the names of all the lakes, rivers and small streams. Roots that were good for medicine or to eat they knew. Flowers and ferns were called by name. The names of all the many varieties of trees, birds and animals they knew.

I was surprised to know from Maxamalinge, the king's son, that every month the king had all the little children of the town before him and he in turn would talk to them, as a great and good father to his own children.

The king would have his servants give to each boy and girl a handful of peanuts. When they were out of the king's quarters there was many a scrap over these peanuts.

I grew very fond of Bakuba and it was reciprocated. They were the finest looking race I had seen in Africa, dignified, graceful, courageous, honest, with an open, smiling countenance and really hospitable. Their knowledge of weaving, embroidering, wood carving and smelting was the highest in equatorial Africa.

PILLARS OF THE STATE

WILLIAM C. JASON

Young people are the life-blood of the nation, the pillars of the state. The future of the world is wrapped up in the lives of its youth. As these unfold, the pages of history will tell the story of deeds noble and base. Characters resplendent with jewels and ornaments of virtue will be held up for the admiration of the world and the emulation of generations not yet born. Others, thoughtlessly or wilfully ignoring the plain path of duty, dwarfed, blighted, rejected of God and man, will be the sign-posts marking the road to ruin.

OATH OF AFRO-AMERICAN YOUTH

KELLY MILLER

I will never bring disgrace upon my race by any unworthy deed or dishonorable act. I will live a clean, decent, manly life; and will ever respect and defend the virtue and honor of womanhood; I will uphold and obey the just laws of my country and of the community in which I live, and will encourage others to do likewise; I will not allow prejudice, injustice, insult or outrage to cower my spirit or sour my soul; but will ever preserve the inner freedom of heart and conscience; I will not allow myself to be overcome of evil, but will strive to overcome evil with good; I will endeavor to develop and exert the best powers within me for my own personal improvement, and will strive unceasingly to quicken the sense of racial duty and responsibility; I will in all these ways aim to uplift my race so that, to everyone bound to it by ties of blood, it shall become a bond of ennoblement and not a byword of reproach.

THE END

NOTES

BIRD, AUGUSTA—Born in Tennessee. On the clerical force of the National Association for the Advancement of Colored People. Contributor to the Brownies Book.

BOND, SCOTT—Born in slavery in Mississippi. Now a wealthy farmer in Madison, Arkansas.

BRAITHWAITE, WILLIAM BEAUMONT STANLEY (1878-)—Author and critic; born in Boston. Editor of "Anthology of Magazine Verse," published annually, "The Book of Georgian Verse," "The Book of Restoration Verse," contributor of literary criticisms to the Boston Transcript and magazines.

BRAWLEY, BENJAMIN GRIFFITH (1882-)—Born at Columbia, S.C. A.B., Atlanta Baptist College, 1901; A.B., University of Chicago, 1906; A.M., Harvard, 1908. Member American Historical Association, American Geographical Society; author, "Negro in Literature and Art," "Short History of American Negro" and booklets of verse. Dean of Morehouse College, Atlanta, Ga.

BROWN, WILLIAM WELLS (1816-?)—Born in slavery in Kentucky. Escaped in youth to the North. Prominent lecturer in America and England. Author of "The Black Man," "Clotelle," "The Negro in the Rebellion," "The Rising Sun," etc.

BURLEIGH, ALSTON W., son of H. T. Burleigh, the well-known composer of music.

CHESNUTT, CHARLES W. (1858-)—Born in Cleveland, Ohio. Admitted to the Ohio Bar, 1887. One of the foremost American novelists. Author of "The House behind the Cedars," "The Wife of his Youth," "The Marrow of Tradition," etc. Contributor to the Atlantic Monthly and Century Magazine.

COPPIN, LEVI J. (1848-)—Born at Frederickstown, Md. Bishop of African Methodist Episcopal Church. In South Africa 1900-1904. Author of "Observations of Persons and Things in South Africa" and a number of religious books. D. D., Wilberforce University, 1889. Ordained to ministry, 1877.

COTTER, JOSEPH S. (1861-).—Educator, author of "Negro Tales," etc.

COTTER, JOSEPH S., JR. (1897-1920)—A youth of great promise who wrote on a sick bed. Author of "The Band of Gideon," "The White Folks' Nigger," "Out of the Shadows."

CROGMAN, WILLIAM H. (1841-)—Born on St. Martin Island, West Indies, A.B., A.M., Atlanta University, 1876, 1879; Litt. D., LL.D., Clark University,

1901. For many years associated with Clark University, Atlanta, Ga., as president and professor. Member of the American Philosophical Association.

CROMWELL, JAMES W. (1846-)—Born Portsmouth, Va. LL.B., Harvard 1874; hon. A.M. Wilberforce University, 1914. Admitted to Bar, District of Columbia, 1874. First colored lawyer to appear before Interstate Commerce Commission. Principal Crummell School, Washington, D.C.; Secretary, American Negro Academy. Author of "The Negro in American History," etc.

DOUGLASS, FREDERICK (1817-1895)—Escaped from Maryland as a slave when a young man. Lectured on abolition in England and America. A noble orator, a clear thinker, and an untiring advocate of the rights of man. Published an autobiography in many editions.

DU BOIS, W. E. BURGHARDT (1868-)—Born in Great Barrington, Mass. A.B., Fisk University; A.B. and Ph.D., Harvard. Scholar; editor of "The Crisis"; author of "The Suppression of the Slave Trade," "The Souls of Black Folk," "Darkwater," etc.

DUNBAR, PAUL LAURENCE (1872-1906)—Born in Dayton, Ohio. Poet; author of "Oak and Ivy," "Majors and Minors," "Lyrics of Lowly Life," "The Uncalled," "The Sport of the Gods," etc. Dunbar stands in the forefront among American poets.

EDWARDS, WILLIAM J.—A Tuskegee graduate who founded the Snow Hill School, one of most important industrial schools of the country. Author of "Twenty-Five Years in the Black Belt," etc.

ELLIS, GEORGE W. (1875-1920)—Lawyer and author. While serving on the American Legation to Liberia, he studied the languages and customs of the tribes of West Africa, and wrote his books on this subject.

FAUSET, JESSIE R.—A. B., Cornell, A.M., Pennsylvania. Associate editor of "The Crisis" and the "Brownies' Book." Author of short stories and verses.

FISHER, RUTH ANNA—A. B., Oberlin College. Has engaged in teaching and social service work.

FLIPPER, HENRY OSSIAN—Served as lieutenant in American Army. Student and translator of Spanish.

FLOYD, SILAS X. (1869—)—A.B., A.M., Atlanta University, 1891, 1894; D.D. Morris Brown College, 1903. Principal of a school in Augusta, Ga. Author of "Floyd's Flowers," etc. Member, American Association Political and Social Science and American Historical Association.

GRIMKE, ANGELINA—Teacher in the public schools of Washington, D.C.; author of "Rachel," etc.

HACKLEY, AZALIA—Musician, pupil of Jean de Reszke. Very successful teacher and conductor of choruses.

HENSON, MATTHEW A.—Began life as a cabin boy. Twenty-three years Peary's companion. He was with him at the North Pole. Thoroughly acquainted with life customs and languages of the Eskimos.

HOLTZCLAW, WILLIAM H.—A Tuskegee graduate who founded the Utica Normal and Industrial Institute in Mississippi; author of "The Black Man's Burden," etc.

JAMIESON, R. C. (1888-1918)—Born, Winchester, Tenn. Educated at Fisk University. Author, contributor to "The Crisis."

JOHNSON, JAMES WELDON—Poet and diplomat. At one time American Consul at Puerto Cabello, Venezuela and Nicaragua. Author of "Fifty Years and Other Poems," "An Autobiography of an Ex-Colored Man." Field Secretary of the National Association for the Advancement of Colored People.

JONES, E. S.—Author of "The Sylvan Cabin and Other Poems."

MILLER, KELLY (1863—)—Born at Winnsboro, S.C. A.M., LL.D., Howard University, 1901, 1903. Dean, College of Arts and Sciences, Howard University. Lecturer on race problem. Member Academy Political and Social Science, American Social Science Association, American Association for the Advancement of Science. Author "Race Adjustment," "Out of the House of Bondage"; wrote chapter on "Education of the Negro" in report of U.S. Bureau of Education, 1901. Contributor to magazines and newspapers.

PENDELTON, LEILA A.—Teacher in Washington Public Schools for many years. Author of "A Narrative of the Negro," "An Alphabet for Negro Children," etc.

PICKENS, WILLIAM (1881-)—Born in Anderson Co., S.C. A.B., Talledaga College, 1902; A.B., Yale, 1904; A.M., Fisk, 1908. Won the Ten Eyck prize for oratory, Yale, 1913. Educator and lecturer. Formerly Dean of Morgan College, Baltimore. Associate Field Secretary for the National Association for the Advancement of Colored People. Author of "The New Negro," "The Spirit of Freedom," etc.

SCOTT, EMMETT J. (1873-)—Born at Houston, Texas. Wiley University, 1905. Secretary of Howard University. Appointed a member of American Commission to Liberia, 1919, by President Taft. Assistant to Secretary of War, 1914-18. Author, "The American Negro in the World War," etc.

SHEPARD, JAMES E. (1875-)—Born, Lehigh, N.C. Author, lecturer, founder of Religious Training School at Durham, N.C. Has traveled in Europe, Africa and Asia.

SHEPPARD, WILLIAM HENRY (1865-)—Born at Waynesboro, Va. Sent by Southern Presbyterian church as missionary to Africa, 1890. Exposed to the Congo atrocities. Fellow of the Royal Geographical Society.

SIMMONS, WILLIAM J. (1849-?)—Born in Charleston, S.C. Boyhood of severe poverty. AB., Howard University, 1873. Educator, editor, minister, author "His Men of Mark" which contains biographies of 177 colored men.

STAFFORD, O. O.—Principal of Lincoln Public School, Washington, D.C. Author of "Animal Fables."

WASHINGTON, BOOKER T. (1858-1915)—Born in slavery. Graduated at Hampton Institute. Founded Tuskegee Institute. One of the foremost educators America has produced. Author of "Up from Slavery," "Working with the Hands," etc.

WHEATLEY, PHYLLIS (1753-1784)—Brought to Boston as a slave in her childhood. Kindly treated and educated; became one of America's well known poets of the early period.

WHITE, WALTER, F.—Graduate of Atlanta University. Assistant Secretary of the National Association for the Advancement of Colored People.

WITTEN, LILLIAN B.—Graduate Smith College. Teacher in the St. Louis High School.